SENECA

His Life and Philosophical Activity

SENECA

His Life and Philosophical Activity

Written by
Platon Nikolayevich Krasnov

Translated by
Filip Poutintsev

Original Russian edition published in 1895:
Сенека, его жизнь и философская деятельность
Платон Николаевич Краснов

ISBN: 9798269412757

Publisher: Filip Poutintsev
poutintsev.com
filip@poutintsev.com

Translation and Introduction: Filip Poutintsev

Copyright © 2025 Filip Poutintsev. All rights reserved.

Cover art: *The Death of Seneca*
by Manuel Dominguez Sanchez, 1871
Cover design: Filip Poutintsev

Table of Contents

Introduction..6

Chapter: I..10

Chapter: II...19

Chapter: III..29

Chapter: IV..37

Chapter: V...46

Chapter: VI..53

Chapter: VII...62

Chapter: VIII..73

Chapter: IX..82

Chapter: X...92

Chapter: XI..105

Chapter: XII...112

Sources...121

Introduction

Platon Nikolayevich Krasnov (1866–1924) was a Russian literary critic, translator, and intellectual who devoted himself to bridging the gap between classical antiquity and Russian culture. Born in Saint Petersburg, Krasnov graduated from the Faculty of Physics and Mathematics at St. Petersburg University; however, his passion lay in literature, philosophy, and classical learning rather than empirical science.

Krasnov published literary portraits, critical essays, and translations, contributing to various journals. He translated prominent classical authors into Russian and wrote works of history and reflection.

His method was characterized by philological precision, moral seriousness, and a belief in the continuing relevance of ancient wisdom for modern life. When he turned to Seneca, Krasnov was not interested in Seneca's biography alone, but in reading Seneca as a moral exemplar – a translator of Stoic ideas into the spiritual struggles of modern times. Krasnov's Seneca works reflect his conviction that Russia's intellectual tradition needed access to classical exemplars – not as remote curiosities, but as mirrors and mentors in moral formation.

Though Krasnov's life was cut short in the early Soviet period, his scholarship remains an example of the pre-revolutionary Russian "classical humanist" ideal: learned, moral, and deeply rooted in the dialogue between the ancient world and the present.

Krasnov's study of Seneca reflects his lifelong interest in the intersection of power and conscience. Through the figure of the Roman philosopher, he explored the tension between civic duty and personal integrity – a theme that echoed strongly in his own generation's moral struggles.

In addition to his historical writings, Krasnov authored novels, essays, and reflections on leadership, virtue, and destiny. His prose is marked by clarity, restraint, and moral gravity. While his later life became entangled with the tragic politics of the Russian Civil War and exile, his intellectual legacy remains that of a disciplined thinker who sought moral order amid the collapse of empires.

Krasnov's study of Seneca reflects his lifelong interest in the intersection of power and conscience. Through the figure of the Roman philosopher, he explored the tension between civic duty and personal integrity—a theme that echoed strongly in his own generation's moral struggles.

In this work, Krasnov presents a detailed and thoughtful study of Lucius Annaeus Seneca, the Roman statesman, philosopher, and writer. Drawing on ancient sources – especially Tacitus, Suetonius, and Dio Cassius – Krasnov reconstructs Seneca's life from his early years and exile to his rise at Nero's court and his final Stoic death. The book is not merely a biography but also a moral and intellectual portrait of Seneca as a thinker who sought virtue amid tyranny and corruption.

Krasnov approaches Seneca from three perspectives: as a statesman, who moderated Nero's cruelty; as a man, whose personal integrity and emotional depth lend warmth and humanity to his philosophy; and as a writer, whose style and ideas bridge the gap between classical Stoicism and early Christian thought. The author pays special attention to Seneca's *Letters to Lucilius*, viewing them as the mature expression of a life devoted to ethical reflection.

Krasnov also traces the legacy of Seneca's ideas, from the admiration of early Christian authors – who saw in him a "pagan saint" – to the divided judgments of later European scholars. The study concludes with an overview of Seneca's reception in Russian intellectual culture, noting translations, interpretations, and the enduring moral appeal of his works.

Written in clear, elegant prose, Krasnov's book combines historical accuracy with philosophical insight, offering a vivid picture of Seneca as both a witness to his age and a timeless voice of moral reason.

Chapter: I

Seneca's Homeland – His Father, Mother, and Aunt – Seneca's Brothers: Gallio and Mela – His Nieces and Nephews: Novatilla and the Poet Lucan – The Family's Shared Talent

The worldwide spread of Roman civilization under the first emperors brought Rome itself the advantage of drawing fresh strength to it from all parts of the world. At first, already in the time of the Republic, Greeks appeared in Rome; then, in the early years of the Empire, Spaniards; later, Gauls and Britons; and finally Germans, who ultimately broke Rome itself. However, no people contributed so much strength to Roman culture, gave Rome so many scholars, poets, statesmen, and even emperors, and all of them with a purely Roman character, as did the Spaniards. The most famous Roman philosopher, Seneca, was also of Spanish origin.

Lucius Annaeus Seneca was born in Corduba between 6 and 3 years before the birth of Christ. At that time, Corduba, as the Romans called Córdoba, was a flourishing commercial city. Conquered and fortified by the Carthaginians, it witnessed the Punic Wars and, from 206 B.C., passed into Roman rule. During the first two centuries before Christ, Corduba was the scene of constant warfare. In the civil war between Caesar and Pompey, it was twice devastated; but with the accession of Octavian Augustus and the spread of peace, Corduba soon recovered and, together with Gades, became a center of Spanish export trade; somewhat later, as the chief city of the province of Baetica, it obtained the right to mint its own coinage. It did not lose its commercial importance even in its later days. However, the commercial pursuits of the inhabitants of Corduba did not prevent them from constantly maintaining abstract interests in philosophy. In the Middle Ages, during Arab rule, Corduba became a center of Muslim learning; the greatest philosopher of that era, Averroes, lived there. Interest in and respect for learning did not die out in Corduba, even in modern times. Thus, even in the last century, visitors were shown as a city landmark the house in which Seneca was born, *la casa de Seneca* [the house of Seneca (Sp.)], and in the vicinity of the city, the country estate where the philosopher's early childhood was spent, *el Lugar de Seneca* [literally: Seneca's place or farmstead (Sp.)].

Seneca's father belonged to the middle, equestrian order of Roman society. It is unknown whether the philosopher's grandfather was a Roman equestrian; it is certain, however, that their lineage did not rise higher than this. Thus, the family of the Annaei was comparatively young; Seneca was what is called a *homo novus* [new man (Lat.)], a circumstance that enabled him to adapt perfectly to life in imperial Rome at a time when representatives of the ancient Roman families were forced either to compromise their conscience or to withdraw from public life.

Seneca's father, Marcus Annaeus Seneca, known in literary history as Seneca the Rhetorician, was a man of remarkable intellect, high education, and rare energy. In the middle of Augustus' reign, he left his native city and moved to Rome. His wife, Helvia, followed him. At that time, the future philosopher was so young that he was carried out of Corduba in the arms of his aunt, his mother's sister, a woman of exceptional distinction. In Rome, Marcus Annaeus Seneca soon found a profitable occupation. Under the first emperors, Roman oratory began to decline and moved from the political rostrum to the school lectern.

Seneca the Rhetorician began teaching oratory and soon gained through this a name, position, and fortune. He was the first to raise the teaching of rhetoric to its proper level and boldly declared that he found nothing shameful in teaching what it was so honorable to learn. Despite a naturally severe character, Seneca was not a pedant and in his books preserved a clear and sober view of the true significance and dignity of the orator. In the works that have come down to us, he caustically mocks the manner of contemporary rhetoricians who saturated their speeches with quotations and rhetorical turns from classical orations to such an extent that they lost their true meaning. Seneca the Rhetorician left behind a collection he compiled of speeches by contemporary school orators on classical themes or on invented legal and moral questions; each of these speeches is accompanied by Seneca's own remarks.

The mother of Lucius Annaeus, Helvia, came from a noble family. The name of the Helvii often appears in the most ancient inscriptions. Cicero's mother also belonged to this family.

Helvia grew up and was educated in the household of her stepmother. Her father, however, took care to give her an excellent education, and she devoted much attention to the arts. Seneca describes his mother as a woman of purity, rare for that time, and speaks with enthusiasm of her maternal feelings. "You will not have to excuse yourself," he wrote to Helvia, "for feminine weakness, for you are free of feminine faults. Shamelessness, which has become so common a phenomenon of the age, has not touched you. Neither precious stones nor pearls could tempt you. You did not regard wealth as the highest good of men. Brought up in an ancient and strict household, you did not succumb to bad example. You were never ashamed to be a mother, although this revealed your age. You never resorted, like other women concerned with their appearance, to artificial abortions. You never used white lead, rouge, or other cosmetics, nor did you wear garments that reveal the body rather than cover it. You considered modesty your best adornment. Toward us, your children, you were tenderly caring. You rejoiced in our prosperity more than you benefited from it. You set limits to our generosity, knowing none for your own, and while preserving our inheritance, you cared for it as your own, yet abstained from it as from something belonging to another. Our successes in life aroused in you only selfless pride. You did not wish to draw any advantage from them."

Helvia's sister, the very one who carried Seneca in her arms out of Corduba, assisted the philosopher both by deed and by counsel at the beginning of his public career. She nursed him during a severe illness he suffered in childhood, and later, when he was already a young man, through her patronage, he obtained the office of quaestor. This aunt was married to Vitrasius Pollio, who for sixteen years served as praetor in Egypt. Despite the looseness of Egyptian morals, she preserved an impeccable reputation and, amid the splendor and luxury of southern cities, led a secluded, withdrawn life. She tragically lost her husband during a sea voyage, but refused at any cost to part with his body and, despite storms and dangers, transported his beloved remains to Rome, where she later settled and became one of the respected women of the capital. Surrounded by the care and affection of these two remarkable women, Seneca spent his childhood. Thus, by birth alone, he belonged to an intelligent and highly virtuous family, in which the high moral qualities of the wife were combined with the brilliant education and energy of the husband.

Marcus Annaeus and Helvia, besides Seneca, had two other sons. The elder, Novatus, later adopted by Gallio and taking his name, distinguished himself in administrative service and, by the reign of Nero, held the responsible post of proconsul of Achaea. We encounter him in the Acts of the Apostles. He is the very proconsul who refused to judge the Apostle Paul, saying to the Jews who accused him: "Jews, if it were a matter of wrongdoing or vicious crime, I would have reason to hear you; but since it is a dispute about teaching and names and your law, see to it yourselves; I do not wish to be a judge in these matters" (Acts of the Apostles, chapter XVIII, verses 14 and 15). Seneca treated Gallio as an elder with deep respect and dedicated to him his treatises "On Anger" and "On the Happy Life."

The younger brother, Lucius Annaeus Mela, lived apart from public affairs. He did not engage in either politics or literature, although he was highly educated and loved reading. Instead, he increased his wealth. His secluded and quiet life did not, however, save him from Nero's greed, and he was forced to die a voluntary death, bequeathing part of his fortune to Nero and his favorites in order to save the rest.

Both of Seneca's brothers, Novatus and Mela, were exemplary family men and devoted sons. Seneca entrusted Helvia to their care during the days of his exile. "Remember my brothers," he writes to his mother. "As long as they live, you cannot complain of fate. Each of them can delight you by his virtue. One, with great intelligence, devoted himself to administrative service; the other, with no less prudence, renounced it. You can always rely on the high rank of one son, on the tranquility of the other, and on the devotion of them both. I know the sincerity of both my brothers' feelings. One sought honors in order to glorify you; the other chose a calm and peaceful life in order to enjoy your company more freely. Fate has taken care that you may find protection and consolation in your sons: in one through his high position, in the other through his peaceful way of life. They will vie with one another in caring for you, and the sorrow over one son will be compensated by the devotion of the other two."

Seneca had no children, except for a son who died shortly before his exile, but his brothers had children. He mentions Novatilla, the daughter of Gallio. At the time to which the foregoing characterization of Seneca's brothers refers, she was a girl of about thirteen and enjoyed great affection from her uncle. Shortly before, she had lost her mother, and Seneca, addressing Helvia, asks her to take charge of her granddaughter's upbringing: "Let her be brought up on your words. You can give her much, even if you serve her only as an example."

Lucius Annaeus Mela had a son, Marcus Annaeus Lucanus, the famous poet, author of the poem *Pharsalia*, who later stained his memory by informing against his own mother, which he did when accused of a conspiracy against Nero, vainly hoping thereby to save his life. He was a handsome, cheerful boy, "at the sight of whom no sorrow could last." In youth, he showed great promise, possessing a powerful poetic talent, but he perished an untimely death.

Besides these two nephews, Seneca probably had other descendants as well. At least some of the tragedies attributed to the philosopher Seneca must belong to one of them.

From this brief characterization of Seneca's relatives, we see that he belonged to a highly gifted family. Almost all its members distinguished themselves by some form of talent. Even the women were remarkably intellectual. However, the spiritual powers of the family reached their highest development, of course, in Lucius Annaeus Seneca himself.

Chapter: II

Seneca's Childhood and Early Youth – His Physical Upbringing – Ill Health – Education – Seneca's Teachers in Philosophy: the Stoic Attalus, the Pythagorean Sotion, the Cynic Demetrius, and the Eclectic Fabianus Papirius – His First Study in Natural Science

Very little information about Seneca's childhood and youth has come down to us. In the historians' accounts, his name appears only from the time when he was already a well-known philosopher. Seneca's early writings have not survived. However, knowing the general character of Roman upbringing, making use of those hints about episodes of youth that appear in the philosopher's works of old age, and finally judging from his character, one can make certain conjectures and at least in broad outline imagine Seneca's life in his early years.

Seneca's childhood was spent at home, and his initial upbringing he owed to women, his mother and his aunt. This is attested both by the deep respect he had for these women, by the general gentleness and refinement of his character, and by a love for women that was rare among philosophers of the Stoic school. In Seneca's writings, women are nowhere regarded as an obstacle to abstract pursuits, as a temptation that must be eliminated. On the contrary, he often mentions, especially about his second wife, Paulina, how much he owed women for the purity of his morals and thoughts. In addition, Seneca was a weak and sickly child, and such children always enjoyed the care of women. In his *Consolation to Helvia*, Seneca mentions a severe illness during which his aunt cared for him.

Seneca's family was close-knit. It may be assumed that in childhood all three brothers lived together with their parents and aunt. The tender friendship that bound the brothers together lasted throughout their lives.

Like most well-to-do Romans, the Annaei family left Rome for the summer. Seneca himself later owned several villas; it is unknown how many his father had. One must think, however, that most often the Annaei spent the summer at that country villa, a few hours' journey from Rome, the visit to which Seneca speaks of in old age in one of his letters:

"Wherever I turn, everywhere I see signs of my old age. I arrived at my country villa and was dissatisfied that its upkeep cost so much. In response to my complaints, the steward replied that he was not to blame, that he, on his part, had taken all measures, but that the villa itself was old. Furthermore, this villa was built before my eyes. What indeed have I become, if stones of the same age as myself are crumbling? Angered at the steward, I began to look for an excuse to find fault with something. 'Obviously,' I said, 'no one looks after these plane trees. Their foliage is sparse, their branches are bent and knotted, their trunks black and uneven. None of this would be so if they were dug around and watered properly.' At this, the steward began to swear that he had done all this, spared no effort, but that the trees were old. However, I myself planted them and saw their first leaves. Looking at the doors of the house, I cried out: 'And what sort of feeble old man is this? It is no wonder he stands at the door; it is time to throw him out of the house. Where did you find such a one? Furthermore, what pleasure do you take in dragging other people's corpses about?' However, this old man said to me: 'Have you really not recognized me? I am Felicio, the very Felicio to whom you gave statuettes of the gods in childhood. I am the son of your steward Philositus, and once I was your favorite...'"

Much more attention was paid to physical development in Rome than among us. Furthermore, Seneca, despite the sedentary nature of his character and his weak constitution, engaged in gymnastic exercises. These consisted of gardening work, running, discus throwing, and above all, bathing in cold water. A favorite place for this among the Romans was the Euripus, a canal encircling Rome with icy water. In childhood and youth, Seneca bathed there all year round; even in winter, on the first day of the New Year, he would plunge into the baths called the "Virgin Waters" into cold, almost icy water and swim there. Having grown old, Seneca chose warmer waters for bathing: first the Tiber, and then artificial baths with warm water. Seneca, as has already been mentioned more than once, was frail in health. By his own words, he experienced almost all illnesses. In general, Seneca had to become acquainted early with doctors and medicines. Throughout his life, he so often had to resort to them that even in his philosophical writings, he frequently uses comparisons and analogies borrowed from the field of medicine. In old age, Seneca suffered from asthma; in youth, besides the usual childhood diseases, he had to endure chronic catarrh of the respiratory tract. "At first," writes the philosopher, "I paid no particular attention to it: thanks to my youth, it was not especially hard for me to bear the illness. However, finally I had to take to my bed, since the catarrh brought me to the point that I wasted away entirely and became terribly weak. I even began to think about suicide, but the thought of how I would leave my aged father, who loved me very much, held me back. I considered not how beautifully I myself might die, but how much he would grieve at my death."

During his illness, Seneca's friends entertained him with consolations, visits, and conversations. Later, Seneca recalled them with a feeling of deep gratitude: "Nothing restores the strength of the sick so much as the sympathy of friends. Nothing removes the expectation and fear of death to such an extent. I did not think that I would die entirely if they survived me. I thought that I would then live, if not with them, then through them. It seemed to me that I would not give up my spirit, that I would not hand it over to them. All this supported in me the desire to recover and patiently endure all sufferings." Philosophy contributed even more to Seneca's patience, being for him not merely an object of study, but a conviction of the heart, which he consciously and consistently carried through in his life.

In general, abstract and scholarly pursuits absorbed the greater part of Seneca's life. He received his initial education under the guidance of his father, the famous rhetorician. Seneca probably also attended some school. In his letters, at least, there are indications that he was well acquainted with the shortcomings of Roman school instruction. Thus, condemning in one of his letters the scholasticism that stifled the Roman school no less than the medieval and the modern one, Seneca remarks: "We learn not for life, but for school." In his other works, Seneca displays extraordinary erudition and knowledge of scholastic authors, which he could hardly have acquired later by studying philosophy only in his spare hours during his legal and administrative activity, especially since he speaks of all these school authors with greater or lesser contempt.

Thus, one can say with confidence that by the age of twenty, when, having left school education behind, he turned to attending lectures on philosophy by the best philosophers of the time, Seneca possessed solid knowledge of the Greek language, grammar, poetry, music, history, and mathematics. This was around the year 19 after the birth of Christ.

Seneca's teachers in philosophy were the Stoic Attalus, the Pythagorean Sotion, the eclectic Fabianus Papirius, and the Cynic Demetrius. At that time, he studied philosophy in a very broad manner. Seneca speaks of all his teachers with great enthusiasm; the lectures of each made a strong impression on him. However, an especially close bond arose between Seneca and Attalus.

Seneca would come first to Attalus' school and leave it last. Moreover, even in the breaks between lessons, during walks, Seneca constantly addressed his teacher with questions and drew him into discussions. When Seneca listened to Attalus' lectures, in which the Stoic exposed vices, ignorance, and shortcomings, the young pupil felt sorrow for the human race, and it seemed to him that his teacher was a being higher than other people. Attalus himself called himself a king, but he seemed something higher still, a king over kings. "When," writes Seneca, "he preached poverty and showed to what extent everything beyond the first necessities is a superfluous and unnecessary burden, I wanted to leave the school a pauper. When he exposed our passions and preached chastity, sobriety, purity of imagination, and advised not to give oneself up not only to improper pleasures but even to excessive ones, I wanted to deny myself food and drink altogether." "Some of his precepts," Seneca informs his friend Lucilius in old age, "remained with me for my whole life. At first, I followed them very fervently, but later, having given myself over to public activity, I lost many of these rules. Still, for my whole life, I renounced oysters and mushrooms, since such food serves not for nourishment but only to stimulate the appetite and merely helps one eat more than the stomach could hold. Likewise, on the advice of Attalus, I renounced perfumes for my whole life, especially since what is best for the body is when it has no smell at all. I also gave up drinking wine and began to avoid baths, considering it an excessive softness to relax one's body with artificial vapors. Other habits, however, returned, although I observe strict moderation in them, all the more so since moderation is no easier than complete abstinence."

A significant influence on Seneca's life and morals was exerted by the Pythagorean Sotion. Having expounded the doctrine of vegetarianism according to the teaching of Pythagoras and the Pythagorean Sextius, Sotion inclined Seneca as well toward abstaining from meat. For about a year, Seneca lived exclusively on plant food. He was already becoming accustomed to it, and it even seemed to him that his spirit had become more agile and his mind sharper. However, at that time, Tiberius began persecutions of secret sects of Jews and Egyptians, which seemed suspicious to the government of the day; an outward sign of these sects was abstention from eating the flesh of certain animals. Seneca's father, who in general did not sympathize with his son's philosophical enthusiasms, took advantage of this occasion and persuaded him to abandon vegetarianism.

Among Seneca's other teachers, the Cynic Demetrius is noteworthy for his proud and unaccommodating character. He was a walking opposition to the entire contemporary way of life. He despised wealth, mocked authority, was repeatedly persecuted for his free speech, and yet adhered to the loftiest principles. "I loved him, Demetrius," says Seneca in one of his letters, "and, casting aside fat snails in purple, I spoke with this half-naked eccentric and admired him, seeing that he felt no deprivation at all. It is easier to despise everything than to possess everything. The shortest path to wealth is contempt for that wealth. Demetrius lives as though he not only despised all things, but had granted others the right to use them." In the time of Caligula, this same Demetrius astonished the emperor by his disinterestedness, refusing to accept from him a very valuable gift. "Did he really think," said Demetrius, "that I would let myself be bought for such a paltry price? To bribe me, his entire kingdom would not suffice." To a courtier who boasted of his wealth, Demetrius said: "I, too, would be just as rich as you if I traded in my conscience." In deep old age, he showered Vespasian with insults, but here the scythe met the stone. This wise emperor contemptuously remarked that he considered it unnecessary to kill a dog that barks at him.

Seneca maintained friendly relations with Demetrius into deep old age, almost until his death.

Finally, Fabianus Papirius was renowned as an excellent orator and a highly moral man. "From his mouth come forth not speeches, but morality itself," said Seneca. Elsewhere, Seneca sets him up as a model lecturer in philosophy for the clarity and smooth slowness with which he delivered his lectures. In this manner, however, Fabianus was prevented from writing well: his style was insufficiently compact, and although his exposition was very consistent, it nevertheless seemed inflated and diffuse. Fabianus Papirius and the Stoic Attalus, in addition to philosophy, lectured on natural history. Under their guidance, Seneca wrote his work on earthquakes, later revised by him and incorporated into his *Natural Questions* (*Quaestiones naturales*). In this work, Seneca examines in detail various ancient hypotheses about earthquakes, which explained these phenomena now by the influence of subterranean fire, now by the oscillations of the world ocean on which the landmass floats, now by the pressure of underground gases, now by a combination of several of these causes. Seneca inclines toward explaining earthquakes as the result of the pressure of gases accumulated beneath the earth.

Chapter: III

Seneca's legal career – Clash with Caligula – The treatise "*On Anger*" – Acquaintance with Julia and exile to the island of Corsica

The young Seneca's enthusiasm for philosophy, and especially for Stoicism, did not please his father. Indeed, the social conditions of that era were unfavorable to philosophy. The fashionable ethic of the time was a light Epicureanism, instilled into Roman society by the graceful poetry of Horace. "Virtue, wisdom, and justice," the representatives of the upper classes of that day would say, "are nothing but empty sounds. All human happiness lies in a good life: eating, drinking, squandering one's inherited wealth. That is life; that is what it means to remember that we are mortal. Days pass, and fleeting life slips away. Why, then, think? What joy is there in being a sage in a life in which pleasures will not always be available, even at the very time when one could indulge in them, when nature itself demands them? To prescribe moderation for oneself is to anticipate death and to deny oneself in advance what it will take from us anyway. You have no mistress; you spend every day sober;

you dine as if you were going to have to show your account book to a strict father. This is not called living, but merely watching how others live. Is it not madness to amass property for one's heir and deny oneself everything, when a large inheritance only turns friends into enemies? The more you leave behind, the more your heir will rejoice at your death. Do not value a whit these gloomy and suspicious censors of other people's lives, enemies to themselves, public moralizers, and do not doubt that a cheerful life is preferable to their good opinion" (from Seneca's letters).

Such was the mood of Roman society under the first emperors. It is therefore not surprising that Stoic philosophers were hated because their example was a living reproach to society; to the government, they seemed suspicious because, condemning the contemporary order of things, they naturally returned in their thoughts to ancient republican forms. Later, the Stoics were expelled from Rome more than once by imperial decrees as harmful people. Seneca himself, in his later works, had to prove in vain that philosophy does not hinder political loyalty. Being thus unsafe, the pursuit of philosophy was moreover considered of little honor. It is therefore not surprising that the efforts of Seneca's father and other relatives were directed toward diverting him from the science he loved. Yielding to the insistence of those around him, the young philosopher turned to legal practice: "Medicine," it was said at the time, "leads to wealth; advocacy leads to honors."

Neither Seneca's speeches nor the cases he conducted have come down to us. However, such a widely read and talented man as he, who moreover had such a teacher in oratory as Seneca the Rhetorician, could not but appear as a bright star among the advocates of his time. Quite apart from the content of Seneca's speeches, which could not fail to sparkle with wit and depth of thought, their very form must have been brilliant. A young, enthusiastic, handsome orator, speaking smoothly and with measured cadence, made a favorable impression on his listeners.

Around this time, Seneca married. Who his first wife was has remained unclear. Even in Seneca's writings, there are almost no references to her. Only in one place in his treatise *On Anger*, written at the very beginning of the reign of Claudius, does the philosopher mention that in the evenings he had the habit of reviewing with his mind the entire past day and weighing his actions, and that he did this in the presence of his wife, who, knowing this habit of his, fell silent during that time. His wife did not live long and died even before the philosopher's exile to Corsica in the year 41 after the birth of Christ, leaving behind a son.

Like most jurists of that time, Seneca combined legal practice with administrative service and, thanks to the patronage of his aunt, at the beginning of Caligula's reign, obtained the office of quaestor.

The quaestorship, legal practice, and the considerable inheritance received from his father, who died at the beginning of Caligula's reign, quickly advanced Seneca in public life. By the end of Caligula's reign, he had already appeared at court. The emperor himself came to listen to his speeches. This attention, however, brought Seneca only troubles. Caligula was a generally abnormal man; in particular, he was distinguished by a morbid envy of talent, at times reaching such curiosities that he ordered the destruction in libraries of the works and statues of Homer, Virgil, and Titus Livius. Caligula imagined himself a first-rate orator, and Seneca's success was for him a personal insult. At first, the emperor mocked Seneca's speeches, calling them school exercises and a "barren desert" (*arena sine calce*). However, when he saw that his mockery in no way reduced the number of admirers of the young orator, he ordered him to be killed. This order, however, was not carried out owing to the intercession of one of the emperor's freedwomen, who persuaded him not to kill the philosopher, since the latter was at that time ill and, according to her words, was soon to die a natural death.

Soon afterward, Caligula himself perished, becoming the victim of a conspiracy. The philosopher, who had already been burdened by the duties of an advocate, after the danger he had survived, abandoned them altogether in order to devote himself to the philosophical pursuits that had long attracted him. Approximately to this time belongs the first of Seneca's philosophical treatises that has come down to us, *On Anger*, dedicated to his brother Novatus.

This work aims to refute the opinion of Aristotle, who held that in some instances anger is not only helpful but even necessary. Seneca examines in detail the nature and properties of anger, draws a boundary between anger and indignation and between anger and irritability, then proves that anger is a special state of the soul, fully capable of being subordinated to reason, and finally sets forth various measures that a person may employ both to calm his own anger and to soothe that of another. At the same time, Seneca does not spare examples both of extraordinary self-control and firmness of character and, on the contrary, of excessive license and irritability. The entire work is imbued with both practicality and, at the same time, high moral purity. Teaching how to suppress anger, Seneca teaches universal forgiveness and love of one's neighbor. "Why hate those who offend us out of ignorance?" says the philosopher. Elsewhere, he reasons thus: "The only thing that can give us peace is a mutual agreement to be indulgent toward one another. This man offended me, and I did nothing to him. However, perhaps I offended someone else or will offend later. One should not take into account some particular day or hour. Even if you have done no wrong, you may do it. Furthermore, therefore, is it not better to forget offenses than to avenge them? Vengeance requires much time, forcing one to inflict many injuries because of a single one. We remain angry longer than we are offended, so is it not better to forgive offenses than to compound one evil with another? Add to this that you will always find reasons for anger if you do not fight it. Now you will flare up at one person, now at another, and from constant irritations, old anger will be rekindled as well. Furthermore, when, finally, will you love? Oh, how much fine time you waste on evil! How much good you could bring both to your relatives, and to those close to you, and to your country, if you occupied yourself with them instead of devising ways to harm your enemies."

Alongside universal forgiveness, Seneca also

preaches the broadest freedom. He laughs at the republicans who lament the free institutions of former times and, at the same time, have banished freedom from their own households. Seneca openly censures these domestic tyrants who shout in frenzy at their families and at their slaves.

All this immediately determined Seneca's position at the court of the dissolute Claudius, who at that time was wholly under the influence of the celebrated Messalina. Seneca found himself in the ranks of the opposition, headed by the ambitious Julia, who sought influence over the emperor. There can be no doubt that Seneca gave her wise diplomatic advice. This circumstance, as well as his generally too liberal cast of mind and his sharp tongue, forced Messalina to look for an opportunity to rid herself of the dangerous philosopher, all the more since his strict way of life during his widowhood was a living and constant reproach to her. With the help of one of the hired informers, of whom there were many in imperial Rome, where informing had become a profession, Messalina accused Seneca of a criminal liaison with Julia herself and thus at once achieved the exile of both people dangerous to her and later even the death of her rival. That Seneca was never Julia's lover cannot be doubted. If this beautiful and intelligent Roman woman had sought adultery above all, she would probably have chosen a younger lover. A sickly forty-year-old philosopher in the role of a Don Juan or libertine seems highly unlikely, especially since from Seneca's works of this period, it is clear that he himself regards himself simply as a victim of intrigue. The Roman historians closest to him, Tacitus and Suetonius, thought the same of him.

Chapter: IV

Seneca's elegies on his exile – Letter to Polybius – Letter to Helvia – Life on Corsica and the scholarly work undertaken in exile

After a brilliant administrative career had begun to open before Seneca, to find himself an exile, deprived of relatives and friends, with the road to the future, as it then seemed, closed forever, was very hard. To this, one must add that in Rome, Seneca had grown accustomed to comfort bordering on luxury, while in Corsica, with its unhealthy climate, he had to endure privations. In Rome, Seneca moved in the company of highly educated and refined people; in Corsica, he had to deal with half savages. It is enough to recall how inconsolably Ovid bewailed his exile in order to understand what awaited Seneca. However, Ovid's pleasures had a more sensual character and therefore could be more easily satisfied in Tomi than spiritual pleasures in Corsica. Moreover, fate did not spare the philosopher's affections either. Having lost his wife not long before, Seneca, only a few weeks before his exile, also lost his only son, who died in his grandmother's arms. Naturally, even Seneca's philosophical steadfastness wavered, and this man of iron, who at the end of his days met death with such cold calm, dissolved into complaints that poured out in several graceful poems. In one of them, he addresses the place of his exile, Corsica, in expressions about himself that were used only of the dead:

Corsica, you once gave shelter to Phocaean newcomers.
Corsica, in ancient times, you were called by the name Cyrnus.
Corsica, you are smaller than Sardinia, yet broader than Elba.
Corsica, many fish swim in your rivers.
Corsica, however dreadful you are when summer comes,
You are still more gloomy when Sirius shines from the heavens.
Have pity on the poor exile, or rather, the buried one.
Let your earth be light for him even while he lives.

In another poem, the philosopher describes the nature of Corsica in the darkest colors:

All in cliffs and gloomy rocks,
A deserted and wild land.

There are no rich summer crops here,
It is deprived of rosy apples.
And in spring, the fields of Corsica
Are not covered with fragrant flowers.
Fountains do not murmur with silvery streams,
Furthermore, no kindly flame delights the eye.
Here, there is only exile, and here the exile is I.

In his grief, Seneca went so far as to be ready to beg for pardon. He resolved to resort to flattery and wrote a letter to Polybius, a freedman of the emperor Claudius, with expressions of submission and reverence toward the emperor whom he had mocked so bitterly both earlier and later. When Seneca was recalled from exile, he repented that he had written this letter and searched for and destroyed copies of it. Nevertheless, though its beginning has been lost, the letter has survived to our time and gave Dio Cassius, and after him, certain German historians, occasion for the lowest attacks on the philosopher.

It is noteworthy that of all Claudius' freedmen, who played such a prominent role in that emperor's reign, Seneca addressed himself precisely to Polybius, the one least stained by base deeds. He was a man of intelligence, educated, and not alien to literature. He translated the *Aeneid* into Greek, and the *Iliad* and the *Odyssey* into Latin. Soon after Seneca's exile, Polybius' brother died. Seeking intercession before the emperor, the philosopher wrote to the favorite a consolatory message on the death of his brother. In this consolation, Seneca expresses those comforting truths that he later repeated more than once in other works on similar themes. He consoles the grieving brother by saying that the deceased has not been lost to him forever but has only gone earlier to the dwelling of souls, where he will meet his relatives; he urges him not to abandon himself to grief because death is inevitable and in any case, sooner or later, had to come; finally, he advises him to seek consolation in scholarly pursuits so that sorrow may have no access at all to the soul of the one who has suffered loss. However, alongside this, which cannot be approved, Seneca, wishing to flatter Claudius, advises Polybius to console himself with the possibility of seeing the emperor every day: "You are ungrateful to fate if you think that while Caesar lives you can weep. If he is alive and unharmed, then you have lost nothing and no one, and you ought not to weep but only to rejoice. If tears begin to cloud your eyes, lift them to Caesar, and they will dry from the contemplation of so bright and glorious a being." Seneca ends his message with the following plaintive words, fully explaining the deviation from straightforwardness and firmness that he allowed himself in his letter: "I wrote all this to you for your consolation, although I myself am in an anxious and depressed state of mind. If my letter does not produce the proper impression on you, and my consolations seem of little effect, consider that I myself am in such a condition that it is hard for me to console others; for I myself am surrounded by misfortunes, and even Latin speech obeys me with difficulty, since my hearing is offended hourly by dialects of barbarian tongues, unpleasant even to those barbarians who have become at least somewhat civilized."

The letter to Polybius remained without consequences, either because the freedman did not wish to extend patronage to the exiled philosopher, or because he himself no longer had sufficient influence at court.

However, the philosopher soon reconciled himself to his fate. He knew how to forget his own grief by sympathizing with another's. Hardly having become accustomed to life on the island of Corsica, he hastened to write to his mother in consolation that his lot was not as complicated as it had seemed to him before. This letter to Helvia, which has been cited above more than once, is one of his best works both for the loftiness of its outlook and for its style. The very motive for which the letter to Helvia was written is highly elevated. Seneca forgot his personal privations and tried to console his mother in the grief in which she only sympathizes. Seneca recalls the words of earlier writers that the burden of exile is softened by the fact that the surrounding nature is always more or less the same and that everywhere we can carry with us our moral self. "Everywhere," says Seneca, "our eyes meet the same vault of heaven. If only I could always contemplate the sun, the moon, and the stars, observe their rising and setting, look upon the sky glittering with thousands of stars, if only I could live in their company as far as a man can partake in the life of the heavens, then it would be indifferent to me what earth is beneath my feet. The country in which I live is not abundant in fruitful and shady trees; deep navigable rivers do not water it; it produces nothing of what men value and yields only a barely sufficient harvest for the scanty nourishment of its inhabitants; there are here neither precious stones nor gold nor silver. However, how petty is the man who is occupied by this earthly vanity. One must raise one's soul there, to the heaven that always and everywhere shines the same; one must set against these conventional goods the true and eternal. The longer we build porticoes, the higher we raise towers, the more spaciously we lay out houses, the more we block off the sky. Let fate have thrown me into a land where a hut is the most spacious dwelling. I would consider myself cowardly and base if I could not console myself with the thought that Romulus, too, lived in a hut. One must strive so that virtue may dwell in this hut. Furthermore, it will be more beautiful than all temples if justice, self-restraint, wisdom, piety, reason, knowledge of the divine, and the human dwell in it. Is the place where so many virtues dwell really insignificant? No exile will seem hard if one can withdraw into it in such company."

Seneca easily reconciled himself as well with the absence of comfort. "I have been deprived not of wealth," he writes, "but of the troubles connected with it. My needs are not great: to have shelter from the cold and food against hunger and thirst. Everything beyond that is demanded by vice, not by necessity."

In such conditions, Seneca lived for about eight years. The lack of material conveniences was made up for by intellectual labor. From the very first year of life in Corsica, Seneca set about actively studying the local nature, customs, and language of the population. He discerned in the local speech traces of many nationalities that had succeeded one another on the island. Then he turned to reading writers and to observations in other branches of natural science. Here is how

Seneca described to his mother his way of spending time on the island of Corsica at the end of the first year of his exile:

"I am vigorous and cheerful, as in my best days. My mind is free of petty cares, and I occupy myself with what pleases me. When I grow tired of more serious pursuits, I read something light, or, hungry to investigate truth, I immerse myself in contemplation of nature. I study the lands and their relative arrangement, then the sea, the tides, then that space between heaven and earth in which thunder, lightning, winds, rain, snow, and hail are born; finally, gradually rising to what is higher, I enjoy the magnificent spectacle of the sky and, recalling eternity and infinity, I pass to the investigation of that which always was and always will be."

These words contain, among other things, the program of Seneca's later *Natural Questions*. Evidently, the material for them was gathered by the philosopher already on the island of Corsica.

Of Seneca's works that have come down to us, apart from the letters to Polybius and to Helvia, not a single one has survived, about which one could say with certainty that it was completed during the philosopher's exile. However, judging from the fact that far from all of Seneca's works have come down to us, and also from the fact that during his absence from Rome, his popularity as a philosopher not only did not diminish but increased significantly, one must think that he made wide use of his forced leisure for writing works in various branches of the philosophy of his time.

Chapter: V

Events in Rome – Seneca's recall from exile – His associates at court – Anicetus and Afranius Burrus – Nero's education – His progress in rhetoric – Study of philosophy – The better sides of Nero's character

Meanwhile, during the seven years of Seneca's exile, the situation in Rome changed substantially. Messalina, who in her debauchery had gone to the utmost limits of shamelessness, fell victim to her own recklessness, and the emperor married for a second time, to Agrippina. Through skillful court politics, Agrippina cleared her path to power, removing and exiling some representatives of the faction hostile to her, and winning others over to her side with favors that at times reached quite impermissible proportions. Thus, in order to secure the support of the freedman Pallas, she became his lover. However, having herself reached the throne, Agrippina wished to secure it also for her son Nero, and to that end began to form a party of her own.

Among those whom she drew to court was Seneca. She recalled him from exile, entrusted to him the education of her son, and raised him to the office of praetor. Tacitus remarks, about Seneca's return, that Agrippina brought back this popular philosopher so as not to be famed solely for her crimes. These words of the historian testify, of course, to the respect and popularity enjoyed by Seneca's name. Agrippina's real motives, however, were of a different kind. She entered into marriage with Claudius not for the sake of unity of interests with her husband, but for the convenience of struggling against him. Agrippina wished to rule herself; moreover, she wished to deprive the lawful heir, Claudius' son Britannicus, of the throne and to place on it her own son by her first marriage, Nero. Agrippina entered the marriage bed not as a counselor and friend, but as an enemy; therefore, her party at court was in essence a strong opposition to Claudius. Seneca, for his part, had already established himself as an opponent of the emperor. Exile could only have strengthened the hostile feelings of the future author of the *Apocolocyntosis* toward Claudius, and Agrippina could count on Seneca as a most devoted ally in her struggle with her husband. The philosopher's intelligence and tact were well known at court; Seneca's popularity also had considerable weight in Agrippina's eyes. She knew that by recalling from exile an unjustly punished sage, she would gain in the eyes of the people. Finally, for Nero himself, to be educated under the guidance of the wisest of contemporaries was no slight advantage compared with Britannicus, who was educated among slaves.

The court at which Seneca was to play a role presented a most wretched spectacle in moral terms. Around the dissolute emperor crowded freedmen and slaves. Agrippina surrounded herself with favorites. It was a crawling crowd of moral nonentities, forever intriguing against one another and behaving toward others with the arrogance of upstarts.

Seneca's closest collaborators in the education of the young prince were Anicetus and Burrus.

The moral character of Anicetus was extremely unattractive. It is enough to say that the plan to murder Agrippina by means of a collapsing ship belonged to him. However, Anicetus was a highly educated engineer and taught Nero mathematics and the technical arts. Burrus was a man of a completely different type. He was an old Roman soldier, hardened by campaigns, courageous, of incorruptible honesty, well educated, though outwardly rather dull and rough. Nevertheless, he was the only decent man at court, and it is not surprising that Seneca became closest to him; from that time on, their names are always found together in history.

Seneca's task was not an easy one. Nero's early education had been neglected, and his natural inclinations were of the lowest sort. It is said that his father, on learning of the birth of his son, remarked that only a monster could be born of his marriage. The first years of Nero's life passed outside the parental home. His father died soon after his birth, and his mother was in exile for participation in Lepidus' conspiracy against Caligula. Nero was brought up in the house of his aunt Domitia Lepida, under the guidance of a barber and a dancer. Later, after his mother's return, he was surrounded by better tutors and, thanks to his natural abilities, acquired some knowledge; however, there was no system in his education, and Nero's knowledge remained fragmentary.

By the time Seneca began his instruction of Nero, the young prince was already making considerable progress in drawing, singing, sculpture, verse writing, music, and gymnastic exercises. Scholarly interests, however, were weak, and in general Nero already showed a tendency toward dilettantism.

Seneca took care to give Nero a fully completed education of the scope accepted in the schools of the time. This meant providing some instruction in the arts, mathematics, the Greek language, geography, and history, and then moving on to the study of rhetoric and philosophy. Ancient Latin literature had by then gone out of fashion, and even in schools it was not considered necessary to read Naevius and Ennius; preference was given to examples of Greek poetry.

To assist Seneca, two learned Greeks were invited: Alexander of Aegae, a Peripatetic philosopher, and Chaeremon. Under their guidance, Nero read Greek poets and retained for life a fondness for Homer. However, at the age at which Nero began his studies with Seneca, twelve years, instruction already turned primarily to rhetoric. In this art, Nero did not show exceptional success, and historians even reproach him for being the first Roman emperor whose speeches were composed in advance by another person, namely Seneca. Nevertheless, thanks to the efforts of his mentor, Nero became sufficiently proficient in oratory that on ceremonial occasions he could deliver speeches, and his first speeches, delivered in the senate still under Claudius, were successful.

Nero's education, however, remained unfinished, since Agrippina opposed Seneca's wish to teach the prince philosophy in its full scope. Nero became acquainted with this highest achievement of contemporary thought only very superficially.

As for moral influence on Nero, given the

composition of the court at that time and the moral qualities of Agrippina herself, it was difficult to achieve any results in this respect. Nevertheless, Seneca did not miss an opportunity to instill virtue in his pupil and tried to do so in the most attractive form possible. Thus, one may suppose that if Seneca's tragedies do indeed belong to the philosopher, they were created at least in part for his pupil. Written entirely not for the stage, they contain many moral maxims close to those that the philosopher advanced in his prose works. The plots drawn from Greek heroic life were meant to attract the interest of the young Nero.

There is no doubt that Seneca soon discerned Nero's nature. He early said that Nero was a predatory lion, who needed only to taste blood in order to reveal the full ferocity of his character; therefore, Seneca, as far as possible, kept his pupil on a tight rein, striving to divert him from harmful and cruel pleasures and to direct him toward more harmless and permissible ones. In doing so, Seneca behaved with his characteristic liberalism and by no means demanded from Nero harsh asceticism or complete renunciation of worldly pleasures.

Nevertheless, for all the savagery and cruelty in Nero's character, especially in his youth, there was much that was appealing. He was trusting, cheerful, loved poetry, took jokes easily, and in general was marked by tolerance. His inclination toward poetry offered some hope, and had Nero not remained throughout his life an incorrigible dilettante, he might perhaps have become a respectable writer. In his relations with Seneca, Nero for a long time showed respect and devotion, and therefore it should not seem strange that the philosopher in turn sincerely became attached to his pupil.

Chapter: VI

New friends – Marcia – Paullinus – Seneca's second wife, Pompeia Paulina – Annaeus Serenus – Fabius Rusticus – Lucilius – Empress Agrippina – Intimate philosophical evenings

Court life and Seneca's administrative activity brought him into contact with many very diverse people. With some of them, he formed closer ties, and they became his friends. In all of these friends of Seneca, despite the diversity of their characters and social positions, there was one common feature: a lively interest in literature and philosophy. All of them were either writers themselves or ardent admirers of literature. Among such educated friends of Seneca, who made up his favored circle, there were also women. Such, for example, was Marcia, the daughter of Cremutius Cordus, known to us from the moving letter that the philosopher wrote to her in consolation on the death of her son. The father of this remarkable woman lived and wrote under Tiberius. He wrote a history of the final period of the Roman Republic, in which he fully expressed his radical views, calling Brutus and Cassius the last Romans. By order of Tiberius, these works were burned by the hand of the executioner, and Cremutius Cordus himself, persecuted by the henchmen of Tiberius' favorite Sejanus, starved himself to death in order not to fall victim to them. His daughter, Marcia, remained constantly at her father's side and encouraged him, and she succeeded in preserving a significant portion of Cremutius Cordus' writings and republishing them under Caligula. The life of this liberal woman was a succession of heavy emotional losses, which she bore with rare firmness. Seneca's letter to Marcia is full of elevated thoughts and beautiful consolatory expressions. Death appears to the philosopher as an inevitable consequence of life and even as a consolation in its sorrows. "Seeing so many mothers distressed by the conduct or fate of their children during their lifetime, how can you grieve," the philosopher remarks, "knowing that your son has escaped the vicissitudes of his age?"

Dissatisfaction and discontent with his court and public activity are constantly heard in Seneca's writings. In another of his letters, addressed to Paulinus, entitled *On the Shortness of Life* and written in the very first year after his return from exile, the philosopher calls life only that time which people devote to the study of philosophy and self-improvement. All administrative, public, and other obligations he considers a barren waste of time. Our life is not short in itself, but we squander it. This is the general idea of Seneca's treatise. All the hours spent at banquets, in domestic quarrels, in disputes, in service, are lost. By contrast, whoever devotes himself to wisdom not only does not lose the present but also gains the past. To his years he adds entire centuries.

Paulinus, to whom the treatise *On the Shortness of Life* is dedicated, was in charge of the grain stores in Rome. He was regarded as one of the most zealous and honest officials. According to Seneca, he cared for the public good as for his own, but in administering it remembered that it belonged to others. This was rare at a time when abuses, bribery, extortion, and embezzlement were the most common phenomena. In the house of this Paulinus, Seneca also met his second wife, Pompeia Paulina, who, according to some sources, was Paulinus' daughter, according to others, his sister. Seneca was at that time over fifty years old.

Nevertheless, his learning, experience, refinement of manners, and taste made him very agreeable in society. He willingly spent time among women. It is therefore not surprising that the young and intelligent Paulina could sincerely become attached to the philosopher, who was twice her age, and marry him. For his part,

Seneca was very proud of his wife. He admired her beauty and her good family, but above all, he valued her intelligence, kindness, and graciousness. The philosopher and his young wife lived, as the saying goes, soul to soul, in complete harmony and love. Seneca touchingly describes how she cared for his health when, having fallen ill with a fever, he nevertheless wished, during an attack, to leave Rome for his Nomentan estate.

"I fled to the Nomentan estate," Seneca wrote to Lucilius, "fled from the city and from the fever that was beginning in me. I ordered the carriage to be prepared despite Paulina's entreaties. The physician said that a fever was starting, which he recognized by the irregularity of my pulse. Then I hastened to depart, recalling that my brother Gallio, having fallen ill with a fever in Achaea, likewise immediately sailed away, saying that it was not his illness but the country's. I said the same to Paulina, who cares for my health. Furthermore, since I know that her well-being is bound up with mine, I begin to care for myself in order to care for her. Furthermore, although my years would give me the right to neglect much, I do not take advantage of this privilege of age, for I always remember that in relation to my wife, I must still be young and take care of myself. Furthermore, since I cannot persuade her to be more prudent in her love for me,

I myself have become more attentive to myself. One must yield to such impulses, and although circumstances may be such that it would be pleasanter to die, one must strive to live for the sake of those close to one. For a virtuous man should live not as long as it is pleasant for him, but as long as it is necessary. Wretched is the one who is incapable of loving a wife or a friend so much as to remain alive for their sake, despite the desire for death. I therefore believe that one should care for oneself even in old age if one knows that one's life is dear, pleasant, and desired by someone. These petty and burdensome cares nevertheless contain a pleasant side, for it is comforting to be so dear to one's wife that, for this reason, one becomes dearer even to oneself. In this way, Paulina compels me to fear and to care not only for her, but also for myself."

Later, we shall encounter even more touching proofs of the mutual love and moral bond between Seneca and his wife.

Among Seneca's other friends, mention should be made of Annaeus Serenus, who held the office of prefect of the city watch. Annaeus Serenus was a cheerful man, took part in many of Nero's banquets and amusements in his better years, while these feasts had not yet taken on the character of debauchery. However, cheerfulness did not prevent Serenus from being a devotee of philosophy. Seneca dedicated some of his works to him. In general, among the Roman youth of that time, Seneca was most attached to Annaeus Serenus. When Serenus died prematurely, poisoned along with all the dinner guests by poisonous mushrooms, the philosopher mourned his friend inconsolably and excessively. Seneca's grief was so deep that later he himself admitted that a philosopher ought to be more restrained and calm.

Among his older friends, Seneca renewed acquaintance with Fabius Rusticus, a friend of his father. Fabius Rusticus composed a chronicle of events in the time of the emperors, beginning it at the point where Seneca's father had left off. This chronicle was later used as material for their histories by Tacitus and Suetonius.

Probably around this same time, Seneca also became acquainted with Lucilius, a Roman equestrian who, thanks to personal merit, was soon appointed procurator of Sicily. Lucilius, too, was distinguished by a love of literature and philosophy, as is shown both by his correspondence with Seneca, in which many letters are devoted to various questions of moral philosophy, and by his didactic poem *Aetna*. Seneca loved Lucilius very much. His letters to his friend are written in an extraordinarily intimate and affectionate tone, although in them one hears the voice of an authoritative mentor addressing a dearly loved pupil. In age, however, Seneca and Lucilius were almost contemporaries.

Finally, among Seneca's constant friends in the last years of Claudius' reign, one should count the empress Agrippina herself. Seneca was her closest adviser and friend, and they constantly consulted about Nero's education. Malicious tongues even spoke of a love affair between Seneca and the empress. These rumors hardly had any factual basis, but in any case, they show that even a fifty-year-old Seneca could be interesting and attractive to women. At the same time, they serve as a good illustration of the morals of the time, when it was considered impossible that a man and a woman could discuss abstract matters in private without at the same time indulging in sensual pleasures. The only sure thing is that the fact of a relationship between Seneca and Agrippina is confirmed by nothing, and indeed, on the contrary, in all those actions in which the empress needed loyalty above honor, she did not make use of the philosopher's services.

Seneca's life in the last years of Claudius' reign and the first years of Nero's rule passed, though in full view of all, nevertheless in relative seclusion. He avoided crowds, rarely attended the theater or gladiatorial games that had then come into fashion, was greatly burdened by official receptions, and used every free moment to turn to his beloved scholarly pursuits. If one recalls that all the philosopher's works were written "in hours of leisure," in snatched moments between lessons to Nero, official receptions, and the fulfillment of praetorian duties, one can only marvel at how he managed to keep track of all newly published books and write so many profoundly thoughtful treatises.

Seneca avoided noisy banquets with the gluttony characteristic of imperial Rome. He did not love luxury, and although he lived luxuriously, he attached no special importance to surroundings. In his fine expression, he ate from silver vessels with the same indifference as if they were made of clay.

Seneca's favorite rest from his labors was when, in the evenings, his friends gathered at his house, and together they engaged in reading some philosophical work, such as the treatises of Sotion, Fabianus, or Sextius. After the reading, disputes and debates arose on various abstract metaphysical questions prompted by what had been read. At these intimate evenings, besides Lucilius, there were many acquaintances of Seneca: Liberalis, the aged poet Aufidius Bassus, Flaccus, and many others mentioned in Seneca's correspondence with Lucilius.

The philosopher's life was, in general, full of intellectual interests, and his figure stands out sharply against the general background of libertines and revelers who made up a significant part of the upper classes of the time. There is no doubt that Seneca's tastes lay outside the court and public life, and that what kept him in office was only the awareness of his importance, his indispensability, and his desire for the public good.

Chapter: VII

The death of Claudius – *Apocolocyntosis* – The start of Nero's reign – Struggle with Agrippina – Nero's affair with Acte – Seneca's wealth

On October 13, in the year 54 AD, Claudius died, and Nero, not yet seventeen years of age, ascended the throne. This change had enormous significance in Seneca's life. From a professor of rhetoric, he became an all-powerful minister, since the emperor himself, because of his youth, could not conduct the affairs of government independently, and Seneca had to guide Nero's first steps.

The first actions of the young emperor were to render the established honors to the deceased Claudius. Claudius was enrolled among the gods; Agrippina was appointed priestess of the new divinity; and Nero delivered a solemn funeral oration written by Seneca. This speech, despite Seneca's customary style and tact, which made him justly considered the best orator of that time, did not make an entirely favorable impression on the listeners. While Nero spoke of Claudius' noble origin, the merits of his ancestors, his personal inclination toward scholarly pursuits, and the peace and prosperity enjoyed by the provinces under his reign, the audience's attention was sustained; but when Nero turned to praising Claudius' justice and statesmanlike wisdom, no one could restrain laughter.

Far greater success crowned, so to speak, Seneca's underground satire against Claudius, parodying the apotheosis of this worthless emperor. In it, Seneca poured out his true feelings, all his anger against Claudius, which in the last days had been sharpened even further by the duty of taking part in the emperor's deification, despite the fact that even the most ordinary apotheosis of mortals, though powerful in this world, was deeply repugnant to Seneca.

Seneca had personal reasons as well for hating Claudius, for his exile, and for the humiliations he had to endure at Claudius' court. But apart from personal relations, he regarded Claudius as a contemptible and wretched debauchee. Claudius was limited by nature, and by the end of his life, precisely at the time when he was chosen emperor, he had completely lost his mind. At Caligula's court, Claudius was the target of the emperor's coarse and insulting mockery. Having become Caesar himself, Claudius lived in constant anxiety, fearing conspiracies, and therefore was cruel to those around him. He was also so forgetful that he would often invite to his table people whom he had executed not long before. After executing his wife, Messalina, he soon began to show signs of perplexity at her absence from the marriage bed. When representatives of one province once came to Claudius with a complaint about their governor, he understood as if they were thanking the emperor for having chosen a good ruler for them and extended the term of his proconsulship for two more years. Claudius had the weakness of personally hearing litigants in the forum, and in doing so, he often delivered judgment, having forgotten to hear the defense. In addition, Claudius was extremely irritable and ridiculous in anger. All these traits of the deceased emperor found an exact reproduction in Seneca's satire.

The satire is written in a mixed form, in verse interrupted by prose, and, in the opinion of critics, is the best example of a light political pamphlet. Dio Cassius reports that it was titled "Apocolocyntosis." This word is a parody of the word "apotheosis." Just as the latter means becoming a god, so the former means becoming a pumpkin, a plant that, among the ancients, served as a symbol of stupidity, as cork does among us. However, in the copies that have come down to us, the satire is nowhere called by that name, and likewise, it does not mention the emperor's transformation into a pumpkin. The content of the satire is that Claudius, after death, [It is noteworthy that the author of the "Apocolocyntosis" does not know that Claudius was poisoned with mushrooms, and in the satire, the emperor dies of a fever.] ends up in the realm of the dead, where he lays claim to divine rank. This claim, however, is denied him at Augustus' suggestion, and Claudius is handed over to one of the infernal judges, Aeacus. Aeacus, in keeping with his characteristic impartiality, condemns Claudius without hearing his justifications, just as the emperor himself had done in life. Claudius is sentenced eternally to perform one and the same useless work, namely, since he was a lover of dice, to throw dice forever from a cup full of holes. This punishment, however, is not carried out, because as soon as Claudius begins the task, Caligula appears and demands him as his runaway slave. Caligula's claim is granted, but he gives Claudius away, as useless, to Menander, the clerk of the infernal court, as an assistant in the administration of justice. At this point, the satire breaks off. All its interest is concentrated in private allusions to persons and events in Rome that now cannot be understood without commentary.

Having buried Claudius, Nero, or more precisely, Seneca, turned to public affairs. First of all, Nero delivered a speech in the senate setting out the program of the new reign. Nero promised to remove those laws that aroused particular dissatisfaction among the people. He promised not to be the sole judge in trials, not to judge accuser and accused in the seclusion of his palace, leaving the decisive word to a few intimates. Nero's court would be inaccessible to venality and intrigues, and his personal affairs would be separated from public ones. The senate would enter into its former rights; the provinces would enter the senate through their proconsuls; and Nero himself would stand at the head of the army.

Thanks to Seneca and Burrus, Nero's promises in the first years of the reign were carried out, and many laws passed through the senate without the emperor: for example, a law was enacted forbidding the taking of fees from litigants for conducting a case; the regulation compelling those elected as quaestors to provide gladiatorial games was abolished, and in this latter law one can discern the influence of Seneca himself; and so forth. When Nero was elected consul together with Lucius Antistius and, at the senate's demand, Antistius was to take an oath of loyalty to the emperor, Nero, remembering that consuls are only co-rulers, equal to one another, released his colleague from the oath. In Rome, because of this act, people began to speak of a return to the golden times of the republic.

However, although all these actions were performed in Nero's name, it was no secret to anyone that Seneca stood behind them. And indeed, when a revolt broke out in Armenia, Rome became alarmed, fearing that the emperor, because of his youth, would not be able to cope with it; but the mere mention of Seneca and Burrus calmed the minds of the citizens. Foreseeing in Nero a bloodthirstiness, Seneca paid special attention to developing in the emperor an inclination toward mercy. He succeeded in this to such an extent that, signing the first death sentence of his reign, Nero exclaimed: "Oh, if only I did not know how to write." In this exclamation, however, there is a share of hypocrisy. Nevertheless, Seneca seized on it and at the beginning of the second year of Nero's reign dedicated to him the treatise "On Mercy," in which he extraordinarily exalted Nero's gentle character and eloquently demonstrated to him the good sides of mercy, citing Augustus as an example, who reached the height of glory and security precisely at the end of his life, when he began to deal more indulgently with his enemies, thereby winning many to his side. This treatise of Seneca, although written according to the rules of Stoic philosophy, is distinguished by an extraordinary simplicity and popularity of presentation. Evidently, the philosopher adapted himself to the age and understanding of his pupil. But besides theoretical advice to be merciful, Seneca also tried in practice to accustom Nero to this virtue, making the young emperor deliver speeches in the senate in favor of citizens who had suffered innocently under Claudius. Thus, at Nero's insistence, Plautus Lateranus, accused of relations with Messalina and deprived of senatorial rank, was restored.

Even if Seneca did not succeed in making Nero merciful forever, it is already good that he was merciful at least at some time. In any case, thanks to Seneca, the first years of Nero's rule were so good that later the emperor Trajan used to say that few rulers surpassed Nero in virtues during the first five years of his reign.

Unfortunately, from the very first steps, Seneca had to struggle against Agrippina, who saw in all measures of a republican character a diminution of her honors. She wished to rule herself in Nero's name, but to allow her this, given her petty lust for power, would have been very risky. Therefore, one of the first tasks of Seneca's court activity was the removal of Agrippina. This was not easy, since she had great influence over her son. Nero called her the best of mothers. She attended, behind a curtain, the meetings of the senate held in the palace. Finally, Agrippina possessed a considerable measure of impudence and attempted to place herself even above the emperor, taking advantage of his youthful shyness.

Seneca's first clash with Agrippina occurred at the reception of Armenian envoys who requested an audience with Nero. Agrippina wanted to receive them herself, but Nero, at Seneca's signal, went out to meet her. Thus, under the guise of politeness toward his mother, he did not allow her the honors of an empress.

Seneca's next clash with Agrippina occurred over Acte. As is known, Nero was married to Claudius' daughter Octavia, but this marriage was not to his liking, and given Nero's passionate temperament, great inconveniences could be expected if his love were directed toward some ambitious court lady. Therefore, Seneca and Burrus breathed a sigh of relief when Nero's choice fell on a modest and colorless freedwoman, incapable of playing any political role and moreover revering Seneca's mind and virtue. Agrippina, on the contrary, flew into a rage upon learning of her son's affection. Nevertheless, Seneca, hoping that the relationship with Acte would protect Nero from more dangerous infatuations, favored her. Seneca's friend Annaeus Serenus assumed the extraordinary role of pretending to be in love with Acte and taking upon himself the emperor's sin. Seneca's entire conduct in this affair is worthy of astonishment. To intervene in so delicate a matter, risking one's own reputation, is something of which only a person with a broad moral outlook can be capable.

But Agrippina could not calm down. In anger, she began to threaten that she would stir up a popular uprising against the emperor in favor of Britannicus, Claudius' lawful heir. When this threat reached Nero, he ordered Britannicus to be poisoned, and Agrippina fell into disgrace. Her personal enemy, Nero's aunt Domitia Silana, with the help of hired informers, accused Agrippina of wanting to raise Rubellius Plautus to the throne. The denunciation was made during a banquet, and it threw Nero into rage. In anger, he wanted to kill Agrippina without trial and to deprive Burrus, as one who enjoyed her patronage, of the post of commander of the guard. But due to Seneca's persuasion, Nero revoked his orders and sent the philosopher to interrogate his mother. Agrippina behaved at the interrogation with rare dignity. "I am not surprised," she said among other things, "that maternal feelings are unknown to Silana: she had no children. A mother cannot betray her children as that base creature betrayed her lovers. If Domitia, by her denunciation, wished only to show concern for my son, I am very grateful to her, but it is only a comedy invented by her in the company of her lovers. Through me, Nero was adopted by Claudius, invested with consular authority, received the throne, and what did that woman do for my son? She gave banquets at Baiae. And for what reason would I start unrest, raise troops, hire assassins? Am I to rule? Whoever is on the throne, Plautus or someone else, I will always have enemies to accuse me not of words torn from me in a moment of anger, in a moment of madness of offended feeling, but of crimes that only filial love can justify."

This speech made a strong impression on Nero. He was reconciled with his mother, and this peace between them was far more dangerous than their former friendship. Nero's sensuality at this time reached such proportions that, in order to extinguish it, he, in the company of court debauchees, carried out revels in the streets of Rome.

Agrippina's removal from court was the apogee of Seneca's power and significance, after which his influence over the emperor began rapidly to diminish and fall. By this time, Seneca had reached the highest civic honors: in the year 57 after the birth of Christ, he was consul. His wealth also increased significantly thanks to Nero's generous gifts. His fortune at this time was estimated at the large sum of three hundred million sesterces. He had several hundred precious tripods alone. This enormous estate required for its management a significant expenditure of time, all the more because Seneca did not leave his property as dead capital. His money was put into various ventures in the provinces, chiefly in Britain, and on his extensive estates, Seneca planted vineyards. He managed his properties partly through trusted agents and partly directly, since he himself was an excellent connoisseur of viticulture.

Chapter: VIII

The Scillius case – Accusations about Seneca's wealth – Letters to Gallio *"On the Happy Life"* and to Serenus *"On the Invulnerability of the Sage"* – The treatise *"On Benefits"* – Seneca's views on slaves

Seneca's immense wealth and Nero's unabating favor toward him naturally aroused envy of the philosopher. One of the envious even came forward against him with public accusations. This was a certain Scillius, who undertook to accuse the philosopher, whether on his own initiative or by a secret understanding with someone among the more influential figures of the faction hostile to Seneca, is unknown. Scillius' past was highly questionable. As early as the reign of Tiberius, he was exiled from Rome for extortion in a court case that he committed in his capacity as quaestor. Later, under Claudius, having returned to Rome, he amassed an enormous fortune by informing, which he carried out both on his own impulse and on Messalina's orders. By his denunciations, Scillius ruined no small number of noble Romans.

When, under Nero, the Cincia law was restored, forbidding even advocates to accept monetary compensation from litigants, and Scillius was called to account for violating this law, he, instead of defending himself, launched accusations against Seneca. According to Scillius, Seneca persecuted all of Claudius' friends in order to avenge his exile. The emptiness of Seneca's pursuits and his efforts to push youth onto the stage led to the forgetting of the few remaining representatives of true oratory. He, Scillius, had indeed been Germanicus' quaestor, whereas Seneca had introduced corruption into the morals of that great man's household. Is receiving gratitude for conducting a trial a greater crime than seducing the noble ladies of Rome?

Furthermore, by what philosophy, what wisdom, what merits did Seneca himself, in the course of four years of Caesar's favors, build up a fortune of three hundred million sesterces? Seneca appropriated the wills of Roman citizens and the estates of wealthy men who died without heirs. His exactions burden Italy and the provinces. He, Scillius, by contrast, possesses a very moderate fortune and is ready to endure anything rather than submit to some upstart.

The philosopher's writings provide the best answer to Scillius' slander, in which the most substantial point is the accusation of greed. However, even this accusation does not stand up to criticism. Seneca indeed lent out his money at interest. Dio Cassius even mentions, as one of the causes of the Britons' uprising in the year 61, two years after Scillius' trial, that Seneca, having loaned his money to the Britons, suddenly demanded the entire debt back at once. Seneca likely did this precisely because of Scillius' accusations, not wishing even the shadow of avarice to lie upon his actions. However, can it really be counted as a crime that a man does not leave his capital lying idle? As for the sources of Seneca's wealth, it was formed exclusively by Nero's gifts.

The emperor was very generous with gifts, especially toward his former tutor, and under Nero's despotism, it was impossible to refuse these gifts. Tacitus mentions that after the murder of Britannicus, Nero divided the prince's estates among his intimates. Among them, obviously, was Seneca. Gifts of this kind had to be accepted unwillingly. In his treatise *On Benefits*, Seneca says outright: "It is not always possible to refuse; sometimes one is compelled to accept a gift. Some gloomy, cruel tyrant may take a refusal as a personal insult."

Scillius' accusation incredibly outraged both the senate and Nero himself. The emperor ordered the decision in Scillius' case to be accelerated. To that end, an accusation was brought against the slanderer for denunciations against many noble Romans that had resulted in the death of those accused. Scillius referred to the fact that he had made all these denunciations on Claudius' orders, but Nero made him silent, saying that he had proof that Claudius had persecuted no one on his own. Then Scillius referred to Messalina, but that did not help either. Why indeed had that woman chosen Scillius as the instrument of her intrigues? The general voice demanded punishment for the slanderer, and Scillius was sentenced to the loss of part of his property and exile to the Balearic Islands.

Scillius' trial, however, made an unfavorable impression on Seneca's friends and relatives. Questions poured in from all sides about the degree of truth in Scillius' accusations. Seneca had to defend himself. In the treatise *On Benefits*, which was being written in the very year of Scillius' trial, one can see the philosopher's justifications in many places. However, he set out his apology most fully in a letter to his elder brother, Gallio, entitled *On the Happy Life*.

"They tell me," he writes, among other things, "that my life is not in accord with my teaching. In their time, they reproached Plato, Epicurus, and Zeno for the same. All philosophers speak not of how they themselves live, but of how one ought to live. I speak of virtue, not of myself, and I wage war on vices, including my own. When I can, I shall live as I ought. For if I lived entirely in accordance with my teaching, who would be happier than I? However, even now, there is no reason to despise me for good speech and for a heart full of pure intentions. They say of me: 'Why, though he loves philosophy, does he remain rich? Why does he teach that wealth should be despised, yet he himself accumulates it? He despises life, yet he lives. He despises illness, and yet takes great care to preserve his health. He calls exile a trifle, yet if only he succeeds, he will grow old and die in his native land.' However, I say that these things should be despised not in order to renounce them, but in order not to be troubled about them. Marcus Cato, praising the age of primitive poverty, possessed a fortune of four hundred million sesterces. If an opportunity had presented itself to increase it still further, he would not have missed it. The wise man does not love wealth, but he prefers it to poverty. He gathers it not in his soul, but in his house."

"Why condemn wisdom to beggary? The wise man may have property, but it must not be taken with the shedding of a neighbor's blood; it must not be seized by deceit or filthy lawsuits. Finally, the wise man will manage wealth better than others. The wise man owns wealth; the ignorant man is owned by it. The wise man gives wealth a useful purpose and finally distributes it. Distributes it? However, why stretch out one's hands prematurely? The wise man distributes it only to the good." Answering the slanderers, Seneca compares himself to Socrates, mocked by Aristophanes. "He stands among the denouncers like a rock surrounded by raging waves. Rage, waves. He will overcome you by his indifference – he who attacks one who is firm and lofty harms only himself. You like to find faults in others? You count other people's scratches while you yourselves are eaten through with ulcers. Very well. Point out birthmarks on the most beautiful body, while you yourselves remain covered with scabs. Reproach Plato for seeking money, Aristotle for accepting it. However, how happy you would be if you managed to equal them, even if only in their faults."

In a letter to Serenus, Seneca considers the extent to which Scillius' slander could be insulting to him. The philosopher proves to his friend that a wise man can be neither harmed nor insulted. "If someone wishes to harm the wise man and makes an attempt, the harm will still not touch the wise man. Harm aims to do evil, but in wisdom there is no place for evil, for evil lies only in vice, and vice cannot be where virtue dwells." Still less accessible to insult is the wise man. "The mockeries and impudences that children say to their teacher no one counts as insults, but as pranks. The wise man relates to all people as we relate to children." These fundamental propositions are developed in the letter to Serenus with Seneca's usual wit.

Seneca's most significant work of this period must undoubtedly be his great treatise *On Benefits*, dedicated to Ebucius Liberalis. In this treatise, he examines various questions of how one should accept and how one should bestow benefits, beginning with the smallest gifts. In the chapter on gifts, we even see a man of the world: so wittily and with such tact does Seneca speak about choosing different presents according to the relations and means of those exchanging them. From this chapter, people wishing to give gifts to their friends can even today draw general guidance.

Seneca's thoughts on gratitude are noteworthy, as a feeling that cannot be demanded by force. Seneca teaches that one should not render benefits with an eye to gratitude, but should render them wholly disinterestedly. Likewise, one should not attach special importance to the moral qualities of those to whom one does good: "Bad people will always exist, and one should not renounce virtue because of them." All these ideas, now commonplaces, were then entirely new, and their dissemination in society naturally prepared ancient Rome to accept the teaching of Christ.

However, most remarkable of all are Seneca's thoughts on whether a benefit done by a slave can be considered a benefit. "Many thinkers distinguish a benefit, a duty, and an obligation. By a benefit, they mean what an outsider gives, that is, such a person as could not be reproached if he did not give it. By duty, what close relatives, a wife, children, perform, who in such cases obey the call of moral duty. By obligation, what slaves give, who belong wholly to their master." "First of all," Seneca remarks, "he who does not allow that a slave can render a benefit does not recognize human rights. For the question is not what someone's social position is, but what his moral worth is. A slave can be faithful, can be brave, can be generous; therefore, he can also render benefits, for this too belongs to the sphere of virtue. Slaves can benefit their masters to such an extent that the latter often live by their slaves' benefactions." Somewhat lower Seneca expresses thoughts even bolder for that time: "He is mistaken who thinks that slavery takes hold of the whole man: the better part of him is exempted from slavery. Only the body is surrendered and subjected to the master; the soul is free. It is so free that it cannot be held even by its bodily prison. Fate has handed over the body to the master: that is what he buys and sells. However, the soul cannot be given into slavery. Thus, the master can receive benefits from a slave, as any man can from a man. Why should a man's person diminish the value of his act, rather than the act ennobling the one who performed it? All men have one origin, and all are equally noble insofar as they are endowed with justice and an inclination to good deeds. He who displays in his atrium statues of ancestors and inscribes their names on the entranceways of the temple is only more famous, not more noble. All have one father, the world, though some from birth are destined for a glorious, others for an obscure life." Thus, Seneca taught and wrote long before Christianity became established in the Roman Empire. It is not surprising that admirers of the philosopher wished to see in him a secret Christian and attributed to him a correspondence with the Apostle Paul. The significance of Seneca's humane views is highly valued even by his fiercest opponents.

Chapter: IX

The death of Agrippina – Seneca's involvement – Request to retire – Romanus's denunciation – The Great Fire of Rome – An attempt to poison Seneca – The One Hundred and Third Letter to Lucilius

Soon after Scillius' trial, Nero's fateful acquaintance with Poppaea Sabina began. From that same day, Seneca's gradual decline also began. The old philosopher could not compete for influence over the emperor with a young and beautiful courtesan. However, the sharp turning point that hastened the philosopher's final downfall was Agrippina's death, in whose murder by Nero, Seneca himself played a prominent role.

When Anicetus' plan to kill Agrippina on a ship that was to break apart at sea failed, and Agrippina, having escaped the wreck, sent word of her survival to Nero at Baiae, he was terribly frightened. Nero expected that Agrippina would rouse the senate and the army, proclaiming everywhere that her son had attempted to take her life, and he shouted that he was lost unless Seneca and Burrus could think of something to save him. They were immediately summoned, and the situation was explained to them. Both were so stunned by what had happened that they remained silent for a long time, not daring to look at one another. It was clear to everyone that one of the two, Nero or Agrippina, had to perish, but no one wished to be the adviser in matricide. At last, Seneca resolved to raise his eyes to Burrus and asked whether he would arrange Agrippina's murder through the Praetorians. Burrus replied that the Praetorians were too attached to her house, honored the memory of Germanicus, and would not dare to touch his daughter, and that Anicetus must fulfill his promise. The latter, without hesitating for a minute, took everything upon himself, and a few hours later, Agrippina was killed.

However, Seneca's role could not be limited to this. The emperor had to be justified in the eyes of the people. Nero withdrew to Naples and from there sent to the senate a letter written by Seneca in which he accused Agrippina of attempting to kill him and explained that, when this attempt failed, she herself took her own life – then followed unworthy slander against Agrippina. It was said that she wanted to seize power into her own hands and command the armies. Having failed to achieve this, she had been arming the emperor against the most noble of the citizens. It was also hinted that the crimes committed under Claudius had not been committed without her participation. In short, in this letter, Seneca tried to convince the senate that Agrippina's death was a benefit for the state. However much Agrippina was hated, this letter outraged the majority of Romans. Their murmuring was directed precisely against Seneca, since, as Tacitus notes, people had already grown accustomed to Nero's own crimes.

The circumstances were such that one had to choose between Agrippina and Nero, and Seneca understood this perfectly. There were many reasons to prefer Nero. Bad as Nero was, it was still better to have him as emperor than a woman with insatiable ambition, unbridled passions, and no sense of shame. Moreover, Seneca was sincerely devoted to Nero. Seneca had a gentle, affectionate heart, and in twelve years of inseparable life with Nero as his mentor, he had managed to grow genuinely attached to his pupil; and though he had a poor opinion of him, he loved him. Seneca's decision to advise the killing rather testifies to the moral courage with which he took upon himself the counsel to do what, in any case, had become inevitable. The posthumous slander of Agrippina was also inevitable in order to prevent a popular movement.

Nevertheless, Agrippina's murder deeply shook the philosopher. From this time, the bright tone leaves his writings, and more and more often there begins to sound in them a note of disillusionment which, as we shall see, by the end of his life reaches sharp pessimism. At the same time, Seneca began little by little to withdraw from court, all the more because the emperor's behavior could not evoke sympathy, and Seneca's influence over him was weakening. Nero began to appear publicly in the role of singer and charioteer, which, by the standards of that time, was considered highly improper. Dio Cassius, and after him German historians, relate that when Nero performed in this way before the public, Seneca and Burrus had to gather a crowd of hired applauders and, lifting their garments and beginning to clap, would give the signal for ovations. Such a story, however, is in complete contradiction both with what Tacitus and Suetonius relate and with Seneca's general character.

Furthermore, to deny the credibility of Tacitus' testimony merely because the source for his *Annals* was the notes of one of Seneca's acquaintances and friends, while Dio Cassius' sources are unknown, scarcely has any foundation. Tacitus relates that Seneca aroused Nero's displeasure by openly reproaching the emperor's performances on the stage, and that he himself began more often to write poetry, as if in order to show Nero what kind of literary works could befit a statesman. On the other hand, in Seneca's writings, there is constantly found an extremely unsympathetic attitude toward the theater, not only toward gladiatorial combats, which he calls barbarism and murder, but also toward tragedy and comedy. The very tone with which Seneca speaks of the theater is irritated, and his own tragedies are deliberately written in such a way that they could not be staged at all.

The death of Burrus, which followed in the year 61 AD, announced Seneca's final fall. It was believed that Burrus died from poison sent to him by Nero. In Burrus, Seneca lost his last companion and kindred spirit at court, and the party that hated the philosopher raised its voice. Informers began to slander Seneca to Nero. The philosopher was accused of piling up wealth in pursuit of popularity among the people, of wishing to outshine the emperor himself with the splendor of his villas and gardens. It was asserted that Seneca claimed to be the only truly eloquent orator of his age, that he had begun to write poetry more often since Nero took up that pursuit, that Seneca was a constant enemy of every entertainment of Caesar, and that he not only denied the emperor's merits in taming horses but even mocked his singing. Seneca wished to persuade everyone that all the good acts of the reign belonged to him, whereas Nero was no longer a child, and it was time for him to free himself from the supervision of a pedantic tutor.

When Seneca was warned of this slander and noticed Nero's cooling toward him, he requested an audience with the emperor and, according to Tacitus, said approximately the following: "It is already fourteen years, Caesar, that I have been with you, and already eight years that you have been reigning. In this time, you have rewarded me with so many honors and gifts that they may be called boundless. I will refer to the examples of great emperors who were before you. Your great-grandfather, Augustus, allowed Agrippa to withdraw to Mytilene and permitted Maecenas to live in Rome as a private citizen. One of these men was Augustus' companion in war; the other helped him in governing the state. Both received recompense for their services. I, for my part, have brought you only the fruit of my studies in the quiet of seclusion, and it was my lot to take part in the education of your youth. You have rewarded me with such wealth that I often say to myself: 'Am I, a modest Roman equestrian and provincial by birth, to count myself among the most influential citizens of Rome? Where is that reason that advised me to be content with little? In what gardens do I walk, what luxurious villas do I possess, what broad fields, what enormous revenues?' I can justify myself only by saying that I ought not to have hindered the manifestations of your generosity. However, we have both reached the limit: you have given me as much as a Caesar can give to his friend, and I have received as much as a friend can receive from his Caesar. Such wealth arouses envy. Envy, of course, like everything mortal, is not dangerous to you, but for me it is heavy, and I must think of myself. As a weary traveler or soldier asks for relief, so I, on this path of life, find myself unable to bear the burden of petty cares about my wealth and ask your help. Take it back and order your officials to manage it. Without turning to poverty, I wish only to renounce the excess of wealth that weighs upon me. I myself will withdraw into retirement, and the time that my palaces and villas take from me I will devote to abstract pursuits. You have enough experience in governing the state. Let old men die in peace. It will serve you to your glory that you knew how to bestow the greatest wealth on men who can live without it."

Nero objected to Seneca. He assured the philosopher that he was still necessary to him, to restrain the dangerous impulses of youth and to help with his counsel in governing the state. As for Seneca's wealth, Nero could only be ashamed that his freedmen were richer than Seneca. If he took back Seneca's wealth and released him, people would say that the philosopher feared the emperor's greed and stinginess. Furthermore, is it worthy of a wise man to seek glory by humiliating his friends? At the end of the audience, Nero embraced and kissed Seneca, concealing, as Tacitus notes, the hatred kindled in him under treacherous affection. Seneca could only thank the ruler. Nevertheless, he began to avoid showing himself at court and even traveled to Rome less often, citing ill health or philosophical studies. From time to time, however, Seneca's name was spoken at court. His enemies could not be satisfied while he was alive, and denunciations were repeated. Thus, soon after Seneca's withdrawal from court, a certain Romanus accused him, together with Piso, of a conspiracy against Nero. This time, Seneca managed to deflect suspicion from himself and turn it onto the informer himself.

Some time later, Poppaea gave birth to a daughter. On the occasion of the safe delivery, a whole series of festivities was arranged. The entire senate assembled to congratulate the emperor's mistress; only the proud Thrasea, risking persecution, did not appear. However, under Seneca's influence, Nero not only did not persecute him but, at the next meeting with the philosopher, declared that he had been reconciled with Thrasea. Seneca congratulated Nero.

After the famous fire of Rome, Seneca donated a significant part of his fortune to the victims. However, since in order to rebuild Rome they began to drain the resources of other cities of Italy and the provinces, plundering chiefly temples and even stealing statues of the gods, Seneca, to divert widespread anger from himself for participation in sacrilege, asked Nero for permission to depart to a distant estate. When this was refused, he pleaded a nervous illness and did not leave his house, receiving no one. This aroused Nero's suspicion, and he ordered the freedman Cleonicus to poison Seneca. The attempt did not succeed, since Seneca had long lived in a manner worthy of a Stoic philosopher, eating only vegetables and drinking spring water.

Was it not this last villainy of Nero that called forth the hundred and third letter to Lucilius, full of bitterness? "Every day," the philosopher writes to his friend, "expect danger from people. Fortify yourself against it and be cautious and attentive. No misfortune happens so often, strikes so unexpectedly, and creeps up so imperceptibly. Before a storm bursts, thunder rumbles. In buildings, before they collapse, a cracking is heard. Fire is announced by smoke. However, danger from people comes suddenly, and the nearer it is, the more carefully it is concealed. You are bitterly mistaken if you trust the expressions on the faces of those approaching you. They have the appearance of men, but souls like beasts. However, beasts are frightening only at the first moment of encounter, and once it has passed, they will not touch you, for only need forces them to attack, and only hunger or fear draws them into battle. For a man, however, it gives pleasure to destroy his neighbor.

"Therefore, always remember the danger that threatens you from people, but remember also what your duties toward people consist of. Beware of them so that they do not harm you, but do not harm them yourself. Rejoice in your neighbor's success, sympathize with his sorrow, and remember what you must fear and what feelings you must show yourself. Acting thus, you will achieve, if not that they will not harm you, then at least that you will not be deceived.

"As far as you can, seek refuge in philosophy. It will hide you in its embrace. In its sanctuary, you are safer than anywhere else. However, do not be proud of it. For many, it served as a source of troubles, those who displayed it smugly and proudly. With its help, correct your vices, but do not expose others'. Do not deviate from accepted customs, so that it may not seem that you condemn what you do not do. One can be wise without boasting and without arousing envy."

Chapter: X

Seneca's moderate way of life – Study of Epicureanism – Letters to Lucilius – Thoughts on death

After withdrawing from the court, Seneca led a life even more secluded than before. Even earlier, he had welcomed festivals and games because they distracted all his acquaintances and petitioners, allowing him to work quietly in his study without fearing that every minute the curtain in the doorway would be lifted to admit visitors. Now he received almost no one at all. Seneca scarcely lived in Rome. He resided constantly at his country villa, occasionally visiting his more distant estates, but he deliberately avoided living in cities. His nerves were exhausted, and he could not endure street noise. Having once visited Baiae, the fashionable bathing resort of Roman ladies, he fled from it the very next day, so unbearable to him were the cries of merchants, the splashing of bathers, and the sight of pleasure boats drifting across the bay with singing passengers. In his travels, as in his private life, Seneca avoided all pomp. At that time, etiquette required a grandee to travel accompanied by a whole train of baggage, a crowd of servants and attendants, with riders, mostly eastern slaves, going ahead to announce the nobleman's arrival and prepare lodging and rest for him. Seneca avoided all this. He traveled with only a few slaves, in an open carriage, and read while on the road. He never announced his arrival in advance, and therefore it sometimes happened that his villas were unprepared to receive him: he had to go to bed without supper and on a poorly made bed. Although the philosopher demanded strict order from his slaves, he treated such mishaps with great good humor. At times, he traveled by sea, though comparatively rarely, since he suffered severely from seasickness and once even had to disembark halfway between Puteoli and Parthenope. In old age, Seneca's illnesses worsened; he suffered especially from asthma, which he even called a harbinger of death.

His constant companions were his wife, his physician, and a few friends. All the more passionately did Seneca devote himself to philosophy. Never did so many works flow from his pen as in the last four years of his life. These included short letters to friends who reproached him for withdrawing from public duties, for example, the treatise On Tranquility, dedicated to Serenus, as well as more extensive works on moral questions, including a large treatise on moral philosophy that has not survived, which is mentioned repeatedly in the letters to Lucilius, and also works on natural science. Seneca not only wrote much during this period; he also read extensively and continued his philosophical education, attending, among other things, lectures by visiting Greek philosophers, although it is doubtful that he could learn much from them. In the final years of his life, Seneca also became thoroughly acquainted with Epicurean doctrine. In the first letters to Lucilius, he speaks of the interest he finds in reading authors from the hostile camp, admires certain of their views, and acknowledges them as genuinely philosophical. The letter to Serenus, On the Invulnerability of the Wise Man, even begins with praise of Epicurus. In general, Seneca was not marked by sectarian intolerance and readily recognized the merits of his opponents.

In the last years of his life, during his leisure, Seneca revised his youthful efforts and his Corsican observations in natural science, supplemented them with new observations and data, and published his Natural Questions, which present an original mixture of factual information and hypotheses concerning various natural phenomena, interspersed with moral and philosophical digressions. Although the Natural Questions do not offer the same abundance of material as the work of Pliny, as a literary work, they are immeasurably superior to Pliny's Natural History.

The most significant work of Seneca from this period is undoubtedly his Moral Letters to Lucilius. These letters are truly the result of a living exchange of thoughts with a friend through correspondence, and not merely a literary form adopted for composition. This is evident from the answers they contain to questions raised by Lucilius, from occasional reproaches for delays in replying or apologies for his own slowness, and from references to minor domestic incidents or mentions of Seneca's travels among villas or cities. However, what is remarkable is that the content of the letters is always abstractly philosophical. In our own letters, we inform friends about household affairs, city gossip, and pass on rumors; nothing of the kind appears in Seneca's letters. He wrote to the procurator of Sicily, a provincial, from Rome, almost from the palace itself, sometimes immediately after an audience with Nero. However, there are hardly any mentions of the emperor, and not a word about administrative news or rumors. Seneca withdrew completely into philosophy. All other matters seemed to him a dull obligation, an unnecessary burden of life. He had become disillusioned with his political activity: toward the end of his court career, he often had to act not only against his inclinations but even against his conscience. From that time on, he saw his true calling in philosophy. To Annaeus Serenus, who reproached Seneca for cooling toward public affairs, Seneca wrote: "Epicurus teaches that the wise man may engage in public affairs if their importance demands it; Zeno, however, holds that the wise man should engage in them unless there are grave obstacles. However, both Zeno and Chrysippus rendered far greater service to humanity by living apart from public business than they would have done by engaging in warfare or governing the state." In many letters to Lucilius, Seneca argues that the study of philosophy should be placed above everything else. In one of them, he declares that he is now occupied with the most important task of all: he is working for all future generations by preserving for them the ideals of moral philosophy.

The motives of the letters to Lucilius were thoughts drawn from other writers, chiefly Epicureans, chance events in Seneca's own life, or in that of his friends. A visit to the theater gives Seneca occasion to reflect on the harm of crowds for the philosopher; the fire at Lyon becomes a повод for reflection on the need to be prepared for the vicissitudes of fortune; a visit to a villa fallen into disrepair prompts reflections on the advantages of old age; the festival of Saturnalia leads to a sermon on moderation and poverty, and so on. Seneca, more than anyone, knew how to philosophize on the occasion of any event. It is no wonder that Quintilian remarked that in Seneca's philosophical writings, one sometimes hears the orator. The form of Seneca's works, and especially of his letters, is of the highest elegance and simplicity. His comparisons are always strikingly apt, sometimes witty, sometimes poetic. His language is concise and vivid, and so filled with profound aphorisms that reading Seneca's works in large quantities at once is extremely tiring. His writings produce such a flood of thoughts that they cannot be read hastily, but must be reread several times. This ability to express one's thoughts so concisely and so precisely is especially valuable in moral philosophy, where, if one does not derive a complete moral system from first principles, as Seneca does not, it is precisely the ability to express a practical moral idea, vaguely felt by everyone, in a form that immediately finds an echo in the reader's heart that is required.

As a philosopher, Seneca belongs to the Stoic school, but the gentleness of his own character and his long study of the Epicureans softened the extremes of that school. Furthermore, it is difficult to say what captivates more in Seneca's philosophy: the loftiness and even a certain severity of his ideals, or the humanity and warmth with which he analyzes human feelings.

As a Stoic, Seneca scourges vice and calls the reader to firmness, self-control, and contempt for life. However, he does not banish the living feelings of friendship and love, nor does he regard tears and sorrow after the loss of a beloved person, which he considers the greatest misfortune of life, as a shameful weakness, provided those tears are sincere and moderate. Seneca preaches poverty, yet he is not opposed to wealth, so long as greed does not become a disease of the soul, corroding morality, and the absence of wealth does not cause suffering to the point of forgetting higher interests.

As a Roman, Seneca valued courage and military valor, but as a philosopher, he was peace-loving, and the military ambition of Alexander the Great calls forth his severe censure.

The correspondence between Seneca and Lucilius began in the year 60 and lasted until the end of the philosopher's life in 65. At first, the correspondence was lively, and while Seneca was studying Epicurus, he managed to write to his friend and pupil about thirty letters. These early letters are shorter than the later ones; each concludes with an aphorism taken from one of the Epicurean philosophers, but worthy in spirit of being called universally philosophical. Seneca calls these aphorisms "daily gifts" to Lucilius and jokes that he has spoiled his correspondent so that one cannot come to him without a gift. The later letters are longer, more abstract, and take the form of small philosophical essays. In the very last letters, disappointment, weariness, and pessimism begin to be heard, reaching in the one hundred and third and one hundred and fifth letters, out of a total of 124, such sharp tones of misanthropy that even Schopenhauer himself might have envied them.

As for the content of the letters to Lucilius, they constitute an entire course of moral philosophy. Those questions considered most important by the Stoics are developed in particular detail. Thus, the letters speak much of poverty, of free will, of the struggle against the vicissitudes of fate, of the immortality of the soul, of friendship, but most of all and most frequently of death, of how one should face one's own death and how one should relate to the death of loved ones.

These pages of the letters to Lucilius are all the more precious because later the philosopher proved by his own death that his preaching was not empty words but a sincere conviction of the heart, consciously carried out in life. Seneca appears as a true teacher of death.

We shall present here the principal thoughts of Seneca on death, both to acquaint the reader with the philosopher's art of expressing his thoughts in concise yet complete aphorisms and because the pessimism that sounds in these thoughts is the final result of all the impressions he carried away from his long, varied, and brilliant life.

In death, there is no suffering, the philosopher teaches. "The cause of the fear of death lies not in death itself, but in the one who is dying. There is nothing more burdensome in death than what comes after death. However, it is just as foolish to fear what you will not experience as what you will not feel. Furthermore, how can one feel that through which one will entirely cease to feel?" (Letter 30). "Death comes: one might fear it if it were to remain with you. However, it must either not come at all, or else be accomplished" (Letter 4). "There is no suffering in death, for there must be a subject to experience it" (Letter 36).

Death should not be frightening, because we already know it: "From the very fact that you were born, you must die" (Letter 4). "We experienced death before our birth, for death is non-being; what it is like, we already know. After us, there will be what was before us. If there were any torment in death, it would have existed before we came into the world. However, then we felt no suffering. Let me put it this way: is it not absurd to think that a lamp is worse off after it is extinguished than before it is lit? We, too, are lit and extinguished. In that interval, we experience some suffering. Outside it, on both sides, there must be complete rest. The whole error lies in thinking that death only follows life, whereas it also precedes it" (Letter 54).

Death is inevitable, and therefore we should not fear it: "We fear not death, but the thought of death; therefore we are always equally distant from death. If one must fear death, one must fear it constantly, for what hour is exempt from its power?" (Letter 30). "Often we must die and do not wish to; we die and still do not wish to. Everyone knows that one day one must die, yet when the hour of death comes, people hide from it, tremble, and weep. However, is it not absurd to weep that you did not live a thousand years ago? Furthermore, just as absurd to weep that you will not live a thousand years hence. It is the same thing. You were not, and you will not be" (Letter 77). "We are dissatisfied with fate, but what is more just: that we submit to the laws of nature or that we submit to us? Furthermore, if so, what difference does it make when you die, since in any case, you must die? One should care not about living long, but about living enough" (Letter 93).

Death is a just phenomenon: "It is unreasonable to grieve, first, because grief helps nothing; second, because it is unjust to complain about what has now happened to one but awaits all others; third, because it is absurd to mourn when even the one who now mourns will soon follow those he laments" (Letter 99).

Death is not annihilation, but only transformation: "Everything comes to an end; nothing perishes. Furthermore, death, which we so fear and hate, only transforms life; it does not take it away. A day will come when we shall emerge again into the light, and who knows, perhaps many would not wish this, if they did not forget their former life" (Letter 36).

Death is liberation from the hardships of life: "It makes no difference when one dies, sooner or later. He who lives is under the power of fate; he who does not fear death has escaped its power" (Letter 70). "Freedom is so near, and yet there are slaves. Know that if you do not wish, you will have to die. So make your own what is in another's power" (Letter 77). "The greatest blessing of life is that there is death. It is important to live well, not long. Often the whole blessing lies precisely in not living long" (Letter 101). "He who has died feels no suffering" (Letter 99). "If one looks at sorrows, life is long even for a youth; if at its swiftness, it is short even for an old man." "He who ended life early is happy, for life is not in itself a good or an evil, but only an arena for good and evil" (Letter 99).

There is nothing in life that binds us to it: "What makes us live? Pleasures? However, you are satiated with them. You have tried everything in life. What do you regret? Friends and homeland? However, do you value them enough to stay later at dinner for their sake? You regret leaving the meat market. You fear death, but isn't your life itself death? However, one may object, we wish to live because we live rightly; we do not wish to abandon the duties imposed on us by life, since we perform them well and skillfully. How? Do you not know that one of the duties imposed by life is death? Besides, you will leave none of your duties unfulfilled, for their number is indefinite. It makes no difference when you end life, provided only that you end it well" (Letter 77). "To look more indifferently upon life and death, think each day of how many cling to life just as drowning men cling to thorny brambles in the swift current of a river. How many waver between fear of death and the torment of life: they do not wish to live, yet do not know how to die" (Letter 4).

Seneca, like other philosophers of the Stoic

school, in teaching contempt for death, advised, in some instances, recourse to suicide. In the letters to Lucilius, there are many examples of courageous suicides, historical or drawn from events contemporary with Seneca in city life. Seneca admires the persistence with which suicides pursue their aim. Particularly characteristic is Seneca's account of the suicide of a certain Marcellinus, who resolved upon it because of an incurable, though not dangerous, illness. "Having divided his property among his friends and rewarded his slaves, Marcellinus died without resorting to sword or poison: for three days he ate nothing and ordered a tent to be set up in his bedroom. There he placed a bath and sat in it for long periods, continually adding warm water, and thus little by little completely exhausted his strength, not without a certain pleasure, as he himself said, akin to that produced by a light dizziness when the soul leaves the body."

It is noteworthy that the death chosen by Seneca himself, as we shall now see, bears some resemblance to the death of Marcellinus.

Chapter: XI

The Piso conspiracy – Seneca's death

Seeing in Seneca a silent protest against his own conduct, Nero could not help but hate him. The very fact that he had once owed so much to the philosopher made him all the more desire Seneca's death. Since Nero was not accustomed to waiting for the natural death of those he did not wish to see alive, he seized the first opportunity to destroy Seneca. The occasion soon presented itself, for court flatterers, knowing how hateful the philosopher was to Nero, did not delay in accusing Seneca of participation in the failed conspiracy of Piso against the emperor (this was the same Piso whom Romanus had denounced earlier).

The last days of Seneca's life, from the moment of his accusation to his death, are described by Tacitus with such artistry that we permit ourselves to reproduce here, with only the necessary remarks, the historian's account.

"Finally, it was Annaeus Seneca's turn to die. His death was especially pleasing to the emperor, not, however, because Seneca's participation in the conspiracy had been proved, but because it provided a pretext to accomplish by the sword what had not been achieved by poison. For Seneca's accusation, the words of Natalis were sufficient. Natalis, the informer who revealed Piso's conspiracy, said that Piso had sent him to Seneca during Seneca's illness to ask why Seneca would not receive Piso, and to propose that Seneca maintain his friendship with Piso by more frequent meetings. Seneca replied that he did not consider frequent conversations and meetings between them to be helpful for either of them, but that, in general, he linked his own safety with Piso's security. One of the tribunes of the guard, Granius Silvanus, was immediately sent to Seneca to ask whether such a conversation had in fact taken place between him and Natalis. Seneca at that time, either by chance or by design, had just arrived from Campania and had stopped at one of his country villas, about four versts from Rome. The tribune arrived at the villa toward evening, ordered the soldiers to surround it, and, finding Seneca at supper with his wife, Pompeia Paulina, and two friends, delivered to him the emperor's command.

Seneca replied that Natalis had indeed come to him in Piso's name to ask why he did not receive him, and that he had referred to ill health and the need for rest; but that he, Seneca, had no reason to prefer a private man's safety to his own, that flattery was entirely foreign to his nature, and that Nero himself knew this best, since he had had far more occasions to experience Seneca's independence of mind than his willingness to oblige. The tribune reported these words of Seneca to the emperor in the presence of Poppaea and Tigellinus, Nero's advisers in his cruelties. Nero asked the tribune whether Seneca was preparing for voluntary death. However, the tribune answered that he could not catch the slightest trace of fear or grief either in the philosopher's speech or in his face. Then an order followed to return to the villa with the command to die. The historian Fabius Rusticus reports that Silvanus returned not by the old road but first went to Faenius Rufus, the prefect and chief commander of the guard, and asked whether he should obey Caesar's orders. However, Faenius Rufus, seized by the general cowardice, advised him to carry out what had been commanded. Silvanus himself was among the conspirators and increased his crimes by bringing Caesar's vengeance to the accomplices. However, he lacked the courage to see Seneca again and speak with him and sent one of the centurions to announce death to him.

Seneca, not at all disturbed, demanded tablets to draw up his will. When the centurion refused him this, he turned to his friends with the following speech: "Since I am forbidden to repay you with gifts, I bequeath to you the only thing left to me, and at the same time the most precious, my way of life. If you will remember what was good in my life, then your steadfastness in friendship will be for you a source of eternal glory."

Seneca's friends burst into tears; he calmed them and called them to courage gently, but with a certain sternness, saying: "Why then were our lessons in wisdom? Where is your reason, which for so many years has been bravely trained to endure the changes of fortune? Is Nero's cruelty still unknown to anyone? Furthermore, whom else was it left for the emperor to kill, after he had killed his mother and his brother, if not his former tutor and teacher?"

Speaking in this way and addressing all present, Seneca embraced his wife and, somewhat moved by the sight of his own misfortune, began to urge her to find consolation in her sorrow and not consider it boundless, but to seek comfort in contemplating the virtuous life of her husband. Paulina objected that she too wished to die with her husband and demanded that she be pierced with the sword. Seneca did not wish to deprive her of this glory, and he also feared that, left without support, his wife might be subjected to worse humiliations. Therefore, he said to her, "I pointed out to you the consolations that life can give, but you prefer to die. I shall not oppose it. Let us die together with equal courage, but you with greater glory." After these words, both opened their veins in their arms. With Seneca, exhausted by old age and a strict way of life, the blood flowed very slowly; to hasten its flow, he ordered the veins to be opened also in his legs and at his knees. Wearied by severe pain and fearing to disturb his wife with the sight of his torment, and also himself afraid of anguish at the sight of her sufferings, Seneca ordered that he be carried into another room. There, with an eloquence that did not abandon him even at the last moment, he summoned scribes and dictated to them much that I do not, however, venture to repeat here.

Nero had no personal hatred toward Paulina and, fearing reproaches for excessive cruelty, ordered that she be saved. At the insistence of the soldiers, slaves and freedmen bound up her veins and stopped the bleeding, though it is unknown whether this was done with her consent. For, since people are inclined to believe only what is bad, some asserted that while she feared Nero's cruelty, she sought the glory of dying with her husband, but when hope of the emperor's mercy was offered her, a desire to live awoke in her. After this, she lived several more years, preserving respect for her husband's memory, but the pallor of her face and limbs showed that she had lost a great deal of blood. Meanwhile, Seneca, since the bleeding in his case proceeded slowly and death did not come, asked Statius Annaeus, his friend and an experienced physician, to give him a poison prepared in advance for such a contingency. This was the poison with which the Athenians poisoned those condemned to death. Seneca took it, but in vain, since his body had already grown cold and the poison produced no effect. Then he entered a hot bath and, sprinkling the slaves around him with water, said that this was a libation to Jupiter the Liberator. In the bath, he suffocated from the hot vapors. His body was taken from it and given to cremation without any ceremonial rites. So he had ordered shortly before his death. This instruction was found among his manuscripts.

In Rome, on the occasion of Seneca's death, it was said that Subrius Flavius and his centurions had secretly decided, not without the philosopher's own knowledge, that in the event Piso's conspiracy succeeded. Nero was killed, and power should pass to Seneca as a man summoned to the throne by the splendor of his virtues. A saying of Subrius was even cited, that Rome would have gained little if, instead of a lyre player, a comedian had ascended the throne. In these words, there was an allusion to the fact that just as Nero appeared publicly as a singer accompanied by a lyre, so Piso appeared as a tragic actor…"

Seneca died in April of the year 65 AD.

Chapter: XII

Seneca as statesman, man, and writer – Parallels with Christianity – How early Christian authors, Romance and German historians viewed him – Russian translations of Seneca

In history and literature, Seneca's significance is remarkable in three respects: he is of interest as a statesman, as a human being, and as a writer.

Seneca's political activity has become the property of history entirely. It was not dazzling; no social or economic reforms are associated with his name. Living at the court of a tyrant, Seneca confined himself instead to a passive role, restraining Nero's destructive impulses; the slightest independence on Seneca's part would have aroused the emperor's suspicions and led to a premature resignation, if not death. However, Seneca's political activity was highly beneficial. It is best assessed by the remark cited above, attributed to Trajan, that few emperors surpassed Nero in the first five years of his reign, and by Subrius Flavius' desire to raise Seneca to the throne. Furthermore, indeed, all the merits of the beginning of Nero's reign must be attributed wholly to Seneca.

As a man, Seneca was distinguished by wholeness and completeness. Almost all human feelings were accessible to him; hence, among other things, the powerful impression his works on moral philosophy produce upon the reader. Fervent and easily carried away in youth, Seneca was not alien even to feelings far removed from philosophy. In his treatise *On Tranquility of Mind*, dedicated to Serenus, Seneca openly admits that sinful impulses sometimes overwhelm him: "They lie in wait for me in order to seize me unawares, like enemies with whom one can neither wage war with open weapons, as in battle, nor live in peace, as in time of peace. I am temperate, I dress modestly, I lead a sober life, but at times the sight of wealth and luxury tempts me; I turn away from it, not with envy, but with sadness in my heart; the thought comes to me whether this palace from which I am leaving is not the true dwelling place of happiness. I do not experience sea storms, but I constantly suffer from seasickness: I am not ill, but I do not feel healthy." By persistent work on himself, by self-education, Seneca in old age attained complete impassibility. However, this was not the cold impassibility of an old man who has outlived his time and preaches moderation and abstinence only because he is no longer capable of living luxuriously; it was the conviction of a heart that had placed its ideals and tastes in an abstract and virtuous way of life. His sincere sympathy and responsiveness toward his friends, and especially his tender attentiveness to his wife, confirm that Seneca preserved the most delicate strings of his heart, sensitive even into deep old age.

In his activity, Seneca was not a fanatic. He did not devote his life to a single defined idea. However, precisely the softness of his character made him especially charming to his contemporaries, harmoniously complementing the somewhat severe grandeur of his Stoic preaching and of a life entirely consistent with it, and above all, a death consistent with it. In Roman history, Seneca will always be a bright, clear ray against the dark background of debauchery and venality in the age of the emperors. Russian poet Apollon Maikov had every right to put into Seneca's mouth the following fine verses:

The Maker gave me reason stern,
That I the universe might learn,
And all I found in self and sky
To distant heirs would not deny.
He sent me vice and hatred grim,
A monstrous, vile, unholy whim,
That like the oak on heights I'd grow,
Through storms made strong by skillful woe,

That in the deeds I strove to seal,
My form, my mark, my iron will.
All is fulfilled. My image cast.
One final chisel's stroke shall last,
And proudly stand through ages vast.

Seneca's personality entirely fits his own definition of those great men who live on even after death in the memory of their deeds and their lives.

But still more important for us is the significance of Seneca as a writer. First of all, his extraordinary productivity and versatility are striking. Not even a third of all the philosopher's works has come down to us; yet what has survived fills three volumes in small print and one volume of tragedies. Besides philosophical treatises, Seneca wrote natural historical investigations, works on viticulture, on geography (a description of India and Egypt), and, finally, poems. Seneca's erudition is astonishing. The form of his philosophical writings, with its clarity of exposition, presents a pleasant contrast to the petty captiousness and wordplay of Greek writers and the obscure exposition of German philosophers. His sincere tone also greatly wins one over. Quintilian reports that his manner of writing pleased Roman youth so much that they did not want to read other authors. Tacitus himself partially imitates his style.

Seneca's ideas are always highly humane and distinguished by depth and knowledge of the human heart. Above we cited his humane views on slaves; one could cite many excerpts in which he speaks of forgiving enemies, of devoted love for one's neighbor. Seneca is one of the most convinced of the immortality of the soul among writers. In the letters to Lucilius there is a passage from which one can see that Seneca's concepts of the Deity and of the Holy Spirit were almost identical to Christian ones. Here is that passage:

"God is near you; He is with you; He is in you. Yes, Lucilius, it is so: within us dwells the Holy Spirit, the guardian and watcher of every good and evil within us... No one can be good without God: who can rise above fate without His help? Only God gives us beautiful and lofty counsel. In every virtuous man

God dwells, though it is unknown which.

If it has happened to you to enter a grove of old trees that have outgrown their ordinary height and in which the sky is hidden by the shade of branches interwoven with one another, then the austere mystery of that place and the awe before such thick and impenetrable shade surely disposed you to faith in a divine presence... Furthermore, if you meet a man who remains fearless amid dangers, free of passions, happy in the most disastrous circumstances, who relates to people as a superior and to the gods as an equal, will not reverence seize you before him? Will you not think of him that this is a higher being and cannot be like that wretched body in which you dwell? The Spirit of God has descended upon him... Just as the rays of the sun reach the earth but always remain where they are sent from, so the great Holy Spirit, having descended upon such a man so that we might more easily know the Deity, though he lives among us, nevertheless gravitates to his source."

It is no wonder that Tertullian found many Christian thoughts in Seneca's writings. Later, Lactantius, having made several excerpts from Seneca, remarks that it is impossible even for a Christian to speak more truly of God than Seneca wrote about Him. Saint Jerome directly includes Seneca among Christian writers and enters him into the list of saints, referring to the correspondence then circulating in society between Seneca and the Apostle Paul. Blessed Augustine also mentions this correspondence, and in the Middle Ages, Seneca was quoted at councils. Upon closer examination, however, it turned out that this correspondence was only the product of school exercises by a medieval writer who knew how to imitate Seneca's style. Nevertheless, interest in and respect for Seneca never died out or diminished among Western writers.

Alongside such fame and praise, there was, however, also a reaction. Quintilian took a critical view of Seneca's style, finding in it signs of the decline of genuine eloquence. Dio Cassius, or rather the Byzantine monk Xiphilinus, through whose epitome this part of Dio Cassius' history has come down to us, subjected the philosopher's public activity and moral character to reproach. Diderot, who is the author of what is still the best monograph on Seneca, explains Xiphilinus' attacks by the fact that, as a representative of the Eastern Church, he wanted to diminish a writer whom the Western Church had almost ranked among the saints. Moreover, Dio Cassius, by his political convictions, considered absolute monarchy the highest form of government. In Seneca's writings, and in his public activity as well, many sympathies for republican forms are expressed.

This double attitude toward Seneca continues to the present day. Most Romance writers admire Seneca both as a person and as a writer and become his more or less passionate apologists, to the point that they sometimes try to deny unattractive but indisputable facts of Seneca's life, for example, his participation in the killing of Agrippina. Most German writers try in every way to besmirch Seneca's personality, and for this purpose not only repeat all of Xiphilinus' slanders, refusing to accept the more reliable and favorable testimonies of Tacitus, but go much further and present Seneca as either a morally insignificant person or an ambitious and self-interested man who stopped at nothing to satisfy his base passions.

The attitude of countless novelists who have described the era of Nero's reign is similar. Even so accurate and impartial a writer as Farrar, in his novel *Darkness and Dawn*, written with the strictest observance of historical truth, gives Seneca a very unfavorable characterization.

Such a strange division in the opinions of Romance and German writers should probably be explained either by the inability of the German spirit to understand Romance virtue and the Romance cast of mind, or by differences in religious and political ideals.

As for Russian writers, with the exception of Apollon Maikov, they have paid little attention to the Stoic philosopher. However, in the first quarter of the present century, Seneca was much translated, chiefly in religious journals, and very often he was given the epithet "Christianizing." At that time, the works attributed to Seneca, *Moral Remedies*, some of Seneca's dialogues (among them *On Providence* and *On the Happy Life*), and the letters to Lucilius were translated.

Some selected letters to Lucilius were translated into Russian comparatively recently, in 1884 to 1887, and printed in the Kharkov religious journal *Faith and Reason*. In 1893, "Selected Letters of Seneca to Lucilius" (50 letters in all) was published in Russian translation in A. S. Suvorin's "Cheap Library". Around the same time, a study of the correspondence of the Apostle Paul and Seneca was printed (in the *Orthodox Review* for 1883). Also translated into Russian by Mr. Alekseev was the *Satire on the Death of Emperor Claudius* (*Apocolocyntosis*).

Sources

1. *L. Annaei Senecae opera quae supersunt.* Edited by Fr. Haase, vols. I–III. Leipzig. 1886–1887.
2. *Tacitus, Annals,* books XII–XV.
3. *Suetonius* (on Claudius and on Nero).
4. *Dio Cassius,* books LX–LXI.
5. *Essai sur la vie de Sénèque le philosophe, sur ses écrits et sur les règnes de Claude et de Néron* by M. Diderot. Paris. 1779.
6. *Geschichte des römischen Kaiserreichs unter der Regierung des Nero* by Hermann Schiller. Berlin. 1872.
7. *Geschichte Roms* by Carl Peter. Volume III. Halle. 1867.
8. *De L. Annaei Senecae vita et de tempore, quo scripta eius philosophica, quae supersunt, composita sint,* written by Alphædus Martens. Altona. 1871. (This book determines the time of publication of Seneca's works.)
9. *Seneca's Character und politische Tätigkeit aus seinen Schriften,* examined by I. A. Heikel. Helsingfors. 1876. (An apology for Seneca based on his writings.)
10. *Études sur la vie de Sénèque* by P. Hochart.

Paris. 1885. (In this book, the author, not entirely successfully, attempts to prove that Seneca was not involved in the murder of Agrippina.)

11. *Études de mœurs et de critique sur les poètes latins de la décadence* by M. D. Nisard. Volume I. Paris. 1834. (The author expresses views on whether the tragedies known under Seneca's name belong to Seneca the philosopher.)

12. *The Philosopher Seneca and His Letters to Lucilius.* A lecture by V. Modestov (*Kiev University News*, December 1871).

Printed in Dunstable, United Kingdom